the little brand book

KALIKA YAP & ERIKA BRECHTEL

This is a work of nonfiction.

Copyright © 2018 by Orange & Bergamot
All rights reserved.

Illustrations credit © 2018 Erika Brechtel

ISBN 978-1718164215
Printed in the United States of America
FIRST EDITION

www.orangeandbergamot.com

A portion of the proceeds from the sale of this book go to Girls Who Code

We would like to thank our families for their endless love and support, who build us up and encourage us to always accomplish the next big thing. You motivate us each and every day.

And to the amazing women entrepreneurs, leaders, mentors and mentees we have met through the years, with whom we have collaborated and served, and shared tears, laughs and kick-ass success stories. Your bravery, vulnerability, passion and grit make the world a better place for the good of all.

*This book is dedicated to our moms,
Ederlina Nacion and Linda Inlay,
for bringing their light into our lives.*

table of contents

7 **intro**

9 **how to use this book**

10 **the brand boss code**
OVERVIEW

14 **the brand boss test**
FIND YOUR BRAND ARCHETYPE

212 **archetype speak**
HOW TO COMMUNICATE WITH
ALL THE ARCHETYPES

214 **about the authors**

the 12 major archetypes

20	**the maven.** OUR TEACHERS	
36	**the brilliant.** OUR INTELLECTUALS	
52	**the original.** OUR CREATIVES	
68	**the idealist.** OUR ETERNAL OPTIMISTS	
84	**the gamechanger.** OUR INNOVATORS	
100	**the explorer.** OUR JOURNEYWOMEN	
116	**the powerhouse.** OUR ROCKSTARS	
132	**the boss.** OUR GO-GETTERS	
148	**the rebel.** OUR CHALLENGERS	
164	**the BFF.** OUR TRUSTED ALLIES	
180	**the gem.** OUR NURTURERS	
196	**the charismatic.** OUR FUN-LOVERS	

the IRL Influencetters

34 **Lauren Messiah**
FOUNDER, THE SCHOOL OF STYLE

50 **Ashley Merrill**
FOUNDER, LUNYA

66 **Christine Dovey**
OWNER & PRINCIPAL DESIGNER,
CHRISTINE DOVEY STYLE LTD.
IRIS AND OPHELIA

82 **Zee Johnson**
FOUNDER, WILDHEARTS PR

98 **Anu Bhardwaj**
FOUNDER, WOMEN INVESTING
IN WOMEN, SHEQ, QRYPTO QUEENS

114 **Liz Arch**
FOUNDER, PRIMAL YOGA

130 **Maryam Montague**
FOUNDER, M.MONTAGUE SOUK,
AGENT GIRLPOWER, PROJECT SOAR

146 **Kat Tanita**
FOUNDER, WITH LOVE FROM KAT

162 **Jeni Castro**
FOUNDER, BRONZED BUNNY
CO-FOUNDER, COFFEE DOSE

178 **Danielle Moss**
CO-FOUNDER, THE EVERYGIRL
& THE EVERYMOM

194 **Amy Eldon Turteltaub**
ACTIVIST & CO-FOUNDER,
CREATIVE VISIONS

210 **Roxy Te**
FOUNDER, SOCIETY SOCIAL
& HGTV STAR

OH HELLO THERE, BRAND BOSS.

We are living in an exhilarating time.

The recent wave of women empowerment has allowed each of us to push ourselves and each other to challenge outdated ways, expect more, be our best selves, and live our very best lives. This is where and when we have found ourselves as we put together this book.

When we hear the countless stories from fellow female founders of harassment, pay inequality, limited opportunity, inappropriate behavior, degradation...and only 2% of women-owned companies get investor funding? It was our call to action.

With our 35+ years of combined experience running our own businesses, we joined forces to bring what we could — our unique knowledge and abilities — to the table: business and branding know-how, for the female founder.

We started with offering learning and connection with a tribe of female founders through content, workshops and events. We were surprised to get push back from potential investors we would meet along the way, advising that we were limiting ourselves with this focus on women...as if there aren't plenty of women business owners out there who need help? (In fact, there are 11 million in the U.S. alone who do. We checked.) Wanting to please everyone, at first we listened. But it did not take long for us to feel at our core, uninspired and inauthentic, having to ask ourselves, "Wait, isn't this why we wanted to do this in the first place?"

And that is Lesson #1: Always stay true to your "why." What's our why?

1 million female founders succeeding
1 million jobs created

The Little Brand Book is our first little contribution (more to come!) to add to the swell. We believe that by providing a simple framework for you to better understand the power in your uniqueness, and how to see it in others, we are giving you the first steps to "work it, own it, bring it" in every experience you create – whether that's with a customer, a client, a donor, a colleague, a team member, a friend, and yes...even a potential more-than-friend ;).

So here we are, back to our original intention...and ~~boy~~ *girl*, does it feel so good.

Let's go!

Kalika & Erika

> **It's important to remember we all have magic inside us.**
>
> *J.K. Rowling*

how to use this book.

We have created this as a quick primer reference guide to help you (your friends, your team) learn how to start leveraging your uniqueness, today and everyday.

first... Read the overview of the **Brand Boss Code** to understand how the 12 major archetypes apply to your life, your relationships, your career and company.

then... Take the **Brand Boss Test** to find out what your major and minor archetypes are. The combination of the two make up one of 144.

finally... Look up your unique **Brand Boss Archetype** and get a few tips on how to work it, own it, bring it! We also recommend reading through the other archetypes to get more tips and understand your fellow Brand Bosses!

for fun... Have your friends and colleagues take the test too! (And take guesses as to which they might be!) Also read up on how to best communicate with them at the end of the book!

HOLLAH!

Look out for **Bonus Material** worksheets and tips you can find on our website: *orangeandbergamot.com/bonus*

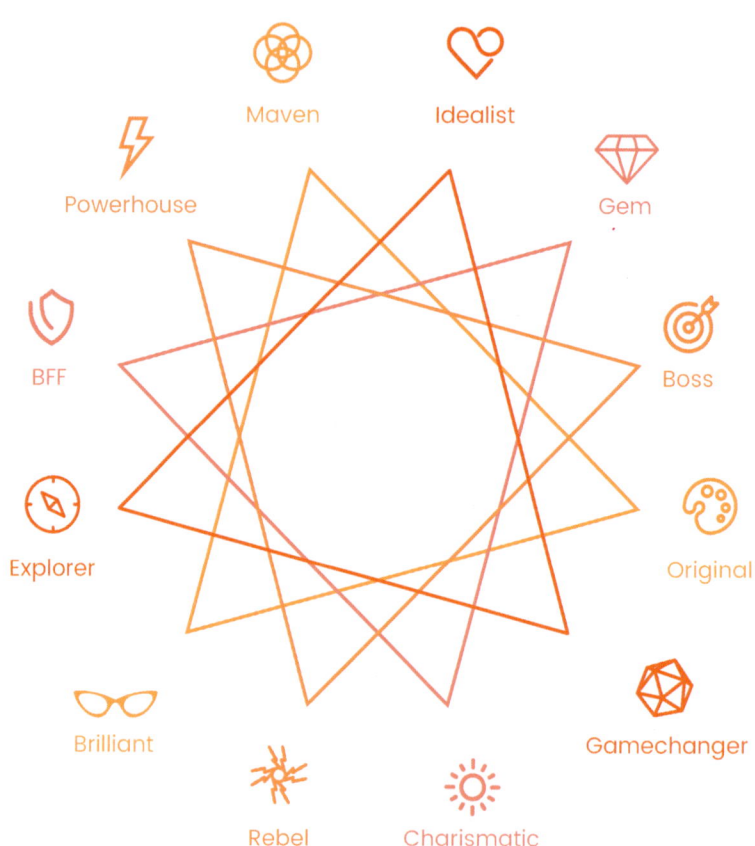

the brand boss code.

Hey you! Do you know who you are? Do you know what makes you unique?

And if so, do you know how to work it to help you be your best self to thrive in business, life and relationships?

Well lucky for you, we do. We know that in today's big world, to be fulfilled and truly successful you first need to be authentic to who you are and know why it matters. Only then can you align with the right audience, build trust and ultimately, brand devotion (a.k.a. your squad, your tribe!).

But in order to be real and authentic, we need to first figure out who we are and what we do best.

The Brand Boss Code is based on 12 major archetypes that every brand fits within. Kinda like when you take that "Which *Sex and the City* Character Are You?" test...are you a Carrie, a Miranda, a Charlotte or a Samantha? Except here, we'll give you actionable steps to *work it, own it, bring it*, every day.

Your individual **Brand Boss Archetype** is a masterful mix of TWO of these 12 personalities — your most prevalent archetype (your "major") and your second most prevalent (your "minor"). Within this framework there are a total of 144 Brand Boss Archetypes. But not to worry! We'll unlock yours and break it down on the following pages.

the 12 major archetypes.

First, let's get to know the major archetypes. They're broken up into four subgroups: the Guides, Optimists, Catalysts and the Woo-ers.

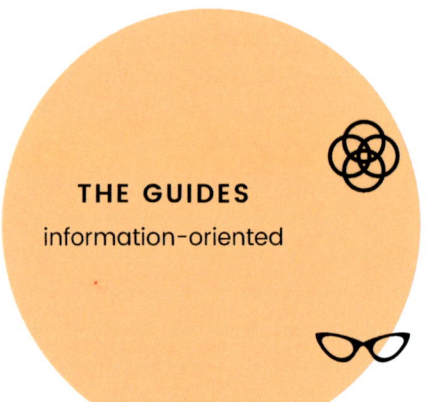

THE GUIDES
information-oriented

Maven
Our teachers. They are considered experts in their fields and get great joy from sharing their knowledge with others.

Brilliant
Our intellectuals. They prefer a quiet corner to a large social gathering and appreciate tangible facts, not intangible emotion.

Original
Our creatives. They see inspiration around them and share it with the world, or use it to create their own.

THE OPTIMISTS
idea-oriented

Idealist
Our eternal optimists. They choose to see and believe in the good of everyone and thing around them.

Gamechanger
Our innovators. They are constantly changing the game with new ideas or methods to improve upon the old.

Explorer
Our journeywomen. These wanderlusters have a natural curiosity and enthusiasm, and love a good discovery.

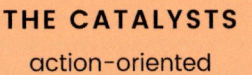

THE CATALYSTS
action-oriented

Powerhouse
Our rockstars of the world. They walk so confidently into a room the rest of us follow in awe.

Boss
Our go-getters. They strive to be the best and look for the best. They feel their best when they're accomplishing goals.

Rebel
Our challengers. They question everything; they're never satisfied with what they're told and instead want to do it themselves.

THE WOO-ERS
people-oriented

BFF
Our trusted allies. We know we can rely on them and quality of their character, and this is what they live and work for.

Gem
Our nurturers. They love taking care of everyone around them, with thoughtful, loving support.

Charismatic
Our fun-lovers. They have a knack for winning people over with their positivity and sense of humor.

the brand boss test.

STEP 1. TAKE THE TEST

Circle <u>any</u> attributes that best describe your brand personality.
The goal is to find in which groupings you have the most attributes.
Take the full test at orangeandbergamot.com/brand-test

1 maven
- Patient
- Spirited
- Intelligent
- Empowering
- Skilled
- Respected

4 idealist
- Passionate
- Optimistic
- Hopeful
- Devoted
- Refined
- Thoughtful

2 brilliant
- Fact-driven
- Inquisitive
- Analytical
- Insightful
- Educated
- Rational

5 gamechanger
- Forward-thinking
- Trendsetting
- Ambitious
- Bold
- Prolific
- Inventive

3 original
- Creative
- Inspired
- Cultured
- Pondering
- Sophisticated
- Tasteful

6 explorer
- Adventurous
- Challenging
- Curious
- Lively
- Eager
- Seeking

*write your results here ⟶

STEP 2. CALCULATE YOUR RESULTS

The grouping in which you have the MOST attributes in is your "major" archetype. The second most is your "minor" archetype. Refer to the following pages to determine your **Brand Boss Archetype**.

7 powerhouse
- Confident
- Problem-solving
- Courageous
- Competitive
- Heroic
- Efficient

10 BFF
- Trustworthy
- Timeless
- Mindful
- Loyal
- Comforting
- Humble

8 boss
- Determined
- Successful
- Productive
- Motivated
- Vigorous
- Hard-working

11 gem
- Supportive
- Sensitive
- Warm
- Communicative
- Kind
- Empathetic

9 rebel
- Adaptive
- Independent
- Free-thinking
- Daring
- Persistent
- Brave

12 charismatic
- Witty
- Humorous
- Positive
- Uplifting
- Entertaining
- Playful

your major archetype:

your minor archetype:

STEP 3. RESULTS: YOUR BRAND MIX MASTERY

1. maven

your major x	*your minor* =	*your archetype* →	*page #*
	MAVEN =	Instructor	22
	GAMECHANGER =	Teacher	23
	IDEALIST =	Hopeful	24
	EXPLORER =	Pilot	25
	POWERHOUSE =	Motivator	26
	BOSS =	Master	27
	BRILLIANT =	Professor	28
	REBEL =	Forthright	29
	BFF =	Sage	30
	GEM =	Mentor	31
	ORIGINAL =	Luminary	32
	CHARISMATIC =	Tutor	33

2. brilliant

your major x	*your minor* =	*your archetype* →	*page #*
	MAVEN =	Philosopher	38
	GAMECHANGER =	Genius	39
	IDEALIST =	Thinker	40
	EXPLORER =	Scholar	41
	POWERHOUSE =	Egalitarian	42
	BOSS =	Prodigy	43
	BRILLIANT =	Academic	44
	REBEL =	Whiz	45
	BFF =	Realist	46
	GEM =	Allocator	47
	ORIGINAL =	Poet	48
	CHARISMATIC =	Geek	49

3. original

your major x	*your minor* =	*your archetype* →	*page #*
	MAVEN =	Curator	54
	GAMECHANGER =	Creator	55
	IDEALIST =	Ponderer	56
	EXPLORER =	Novelist	57
	POWERHOUSE =	Celestial	58
	BOSS =	Composer	59
	BRILLIANT =	Architect	60
	REBEL =	Rule-breaker	61
	BFF =	Classicist	62
	GEM =	Affectionate	63
	ORIGINAL =	Virtuoso	64
	CHARISMATIC =	Playful	65

4 idealist

your major	x	your minor	=	your archetype	→	page #
		MAVEN	=	Utopian		70
		GAMECHANGER	=	Optimist		71
		IDEALIST	=	Lover		72
		EXPLORER	=	Seeker		73
		POWERHOUSE	=	Gladiator		74
		BOSS	=	Elegant		75
		BRILLIANT	=	Fox		76
		REBEL	=	Paramour		77
		BFF	=	Romantic		78
		GEM	=	Passionate		79
		ORIGINAL	=	Muse		80
		CHARISMATIC	=	Whimsical		81

5 gamechanger

your major	x	your minor	=	your archetype	→	page #
		MAVEN	=	Groundbreaker		86
		GAMECHANGER	=	Trendsetter		87
		IDEALIST	=	Dreamer		88
		EXPLORER	=	Pathfinder		89
		POWERHOUSE	=	Influencer		90
		BOSS	=	Pioneer		91
		BRILLIANT	=	Strategist		92
		REBEL	=	Maverick		93
		BFF	=	Admired		94
		GEM	=	Philanthropist		95
		ORIGINAL	=	Avant-Garde		96
		CHARISMATIC	=	Visionary		97

6 explorer

your major	x	your minor	=	your archetype	→	page #
		MAVEN	=	Scout		102
		GAMECHANGER	=	Inventor		103
		IDEALIST	=	Open Mind		104
		EXPLORER	=	Adventurer		105
		POWERHOUSE	=	Critic		106
		BOSS	=	Climber		107
		BRILLIANT	=	Scientist		108
		REBEL	=	Inquisitor		109
		BFF	=	Inspector		110
		GEM	=	Conscientious		111
		ORIGINAL	=	Animator		112
		CHARISMATIC	=	Bright Spot		113

7 powerhouse

your major	x	your minor	=	your archetype	→ page #
		MAVEN	=	Coach	118
		GAMECHANGER	=	Crusader	119
		IDEALIST	=	Connector	120
		EXPLORER	=	Captain	121
		POWERHOUSE	=	Queen	122
		BOSS	=	Mogul	123
		BRILLIANT	=	Ambassador	124
		REBEL	=	Demagogue	125
		BFF	=	CEO	126
		GEM	=	Advocate	127
		ORIGINAL	=	Director	128
		CHARISMATIC	=	Charmer	129

8 boss

your major	x	your minor	=	your archetype	→ page #
		MAVEN	=	Role Model	134
		GAMECHANGER	=	Tastemaker	135
		IDEALIST	=	Exceptional	136
		EXPLORER	=	Venturer	137
		POWERHOUSE	=	Champion	138
		BOSS	=	Paragon	139
		BRILLIANT	=	Highbrow	140
		REBEL	=	Individualist	141
		BFF	=	Pragmatist	142
		GEM	=	Upholder	143
		ORIGINAL	=	Mastermind	144
		CHARISMATIC	=	Shining Star	145

9 rebel

your major	x	your minor	=	your archetype	→ page #
		MAVEN	=	Icon	150
		GAMECHANGER	=	Revolutionary	151
		IDEALIST	=	Lone Wolf	152
		EXPLORER	=	Experimenter	153
		POWERHOUSE	=	Antihero	154
		BOSS	=	Entrepreneur	155
		BRILLIANT	=	Daredevil	156
		REBEL	=	Nonconformist	157
		BFF	=	Resilient	158
		GEM	=	Rebel with a Cause	159
		ORIGINAL	=	Eccentric	160
		CHARISMATIC	=	Satirist	161

10 BFF

your major	x	your minor	=	your archetype	→	page #
		MAVEN	=	Principal		166
		GAMECHANGER	=	Innovator		167
		IDEALIST	=	Anchor		168
		EXPLORER	=	Researcher		169
		POWERHOUSE	=	Sheriff		170
		BOSS	=	Dependable		171
		BRILLIANT	=	Level Head		172
		REBEL	=	Underdog		173
		BFF	=	Traditionalist		174
		GEM	=	Mainstay		175
		ORIGINAL	=	Artisan		176
		CHARISMATIC	=	Popular		177

11 gem

your major	x	your minor	=	your archetype	→	page #
		MAVEN	=	Counselor		182
		GAMECHANGER	=	Ally		183
		IDEALIST	=	Companion		184
		EXPLORER	=	Cultivator		185
		POWERHOUSE	=	Altruist		186
		BOSS	=	Benefactor		187
		BRILLIANT	=	Trainer		188
		REBEL	=	Tough Lover		189
		BFF	=	Good Samaritan		190
		GEM	=	Humanitarian		191
		ORIGINAL	=	Hippie		192
		CHARISMATIC	=	Glow		193

12 charismatic

your major	x	your minor	=	your archetype	→	page #
		MAVEN	=	Friend		198
		GAMECHANGER	=	Modernist		199
		IDEALIST	=	Light-Hearted		200
		EXPLORER	=	Open Heart		201
		POWERHOUSE	=	Genuine		202
		BOSS	=	Endurer		203
		BRILLIANT	=	Wit		204
		REBEL	=	Anarchist		205
		BFF	=	Congenial		206
		GEM	=	Crystal		207
		ORIGINAL	=	Humorist		208
		CHARISMATIC	=	Comic		209

"When you learn, teach. When you get, give." Maya Angelou

EMPOWERING

enthusiastic

Emotionally Intelligent

Experienced

Respected

Channel your inner:

Oprah

MAJOR ARCHETYPE

the maven

1

You are considered an expert in your field. Your main passion is sharing your expertise with others. Whether it's through demonstration or simple information sharing, you love passing along 'a-ha' moments through knowledge people didn't have before. Seeing it "land" on them and their eyes light up with excitement gives you the greatest joy.

X MAVEN	=	Instructor
X GAMECHANGER	=	Teacher
X IDEALIST	=	Hopeful
X EXPLORER	=	Pilot
X POWERHOUSE	=	Motivator
X BOSS	=	Master
X BRILLIANT	=	Professor
X REBEL	=	Forthright
X BFF	=	Sage
X GEM	=	Mentor
X ORIGINAL	=	Luminary
X CHARISMATIC	=	Tutor

Your Brand Mix Mastery:

 MAVEN x MAVEN

the instructor.

You are 100% Maven at heart. Your #1 goal is to promote the spread of knowledge, and there's nothing you love more than teaching someone something new. When people have questions about the field in which you work, they always come to you.

Work it

You are powerful because you are:
- Fact-oriented
- Patient
- Organized
- Good at public speaking
- Trustworthy

Own it

Get inspired by these kindred brands:

The Smithsonian - Eva Moskowitz

Bring it

Amplify your strengths:
- Write an article or share a tip from your vast expertise via social media. It will make your knowledge accessible for those who want to learn from you.

MAVEN
x Maven

Your Brand Mix Mastery:

the teacher.

You believe the best way to make a positive impact on the future is to instruct those who are a part of it; as a result, you're an active participant in educating the next generation. You use practical yet innovative teaching methods to maximize the results of your instruction.

Work it

You are powerful because you are:
- Hopeful
- Creative
- Devoted
- Knowledgeable
- Good at explaining concepts in a digestible way

Own it

Get inspired by these kindred brands:

Maria Montessori - Bill & Melinda Gates Foundation

Bring it

Amplify your strengths:
- Brainstorm innovative ways you can share your knowledge and connect with others using the latest technology and trends.

MAVEN
x Gamechanger

Your Brand Mix Mastery:

the hopeful.

You're committed to educating others because of the positive way in which you view the future. You know that the more enlightened people are, the more equipped they can be to create a world around them that is better for everyone.

Work it

You are powerful because you are:

- Optimistic
- A part of something bigger than yourself
- Keen to share your knowledge with the world
- Understanding that everyone learns differently
- Empathetic

Own it

Get inspired by these kindred brands:

TED Talks - Marianne Williamson

Bring it

Amplify your strengths:

- Always be encouraging and positive in your voice when crafting your messages; you'll attract others with your positivity.

MAVEN
x Idealist

Your Brand Mix Mastery:

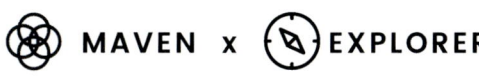 MAVEN x EXPLORER

the pilot.

Knowledge is power, and you feel that your brand is best equipped when it's able to share valuable information with others in order to assist them in their own journeys. You're inspired by the pursuit and exploration of wisdom.

Work it

You are powerful because you are:

- Supportive of research, exploration, and analysis
- Encouraging of others to continue their education
- Thoughtful in teaching others what you know
- Excited about the future of science, culture, arts
- Inquisitive

Own it

Get inspired by these kindred brands:

Deepak Chopra - Travel Channel

Bring it

Amplify your strengths:

- Volunteer to give a talk at a conference or be a docent at your local museum or exploratorium to take others on a journey of discovery.

MAVEN x Explorer

Your Brand Mix Mastery:

 MAVEN x POWERHOUSE

the motivator.

You're very much a role model for others. People are attracted to you because they're inspired by your strength and confidence; you're a fantastic instructor, but your can-do attitude and accomplishments are icing on the cake.

Work it

You are powerful because you are:

- Inspiring
- Bold
- Passionate
- Accomplished
- A leader by example

Own it

Get inspired by these kindred brands:

Maya Angelou - The Zoe Report

Bring it

Amplify your strengths:

- Write down adjectives that would be the embodiment of the message you want to share; live that and be vocal about it, encouraging others through your words and actions.

MAVEN
x Powerhouse

Your Brand Mix Mastery:

 MAVEN x BOSS

the master.

Whether it was through trial and error, persistent learning, observation, or all of the above, you know just about everything there is to know about your specific interest. People consistently come to you for your expertise, which is considered of the highest level.

Work it

You are powerful because you are:
- Eager to spread your knowledge
- Level-headed
- Self-assured
- An expert in your field
- Accomplished

Own it

Get inspired by these kindred brands:

Dalai Lama - Masterclass

Bring it

Amplify your strengths:
- Write a book or column, or start a podcast; share your expertise and connect with your audience through interviews and in-person events.

Your Brand Mix Mastery:

 MAVEN x BRILLIANT

the professor.

You're a bit of a nerd — you love teaching people bits of information just as much as you love learning new ones. You're studious and dedicated, yet visibly passionate about your area of expertise.

Work it

You are powerful because you are:

- Analytical
- Insightful
- Committed to a project once started
- Eager to learn
- Passionate about teaching others what you know

Own it

Get inspired by these kindred brands:

Neil deGrasse Tyson - *The New Yorker*

Bring it

Amplify your strengths:

- Don't assume others know what you know; break it down into bite-size bits that are easily digestible, such as in list form or a step-by-step.

MAVEN x Brilliant

Your Brand Mix Mastery:

 MAVEN x REBEL

the forthright.

One of your highest virtues is honesty — you're known for telling it how it is, even if what you have to say isn't necessarily what they want to hear. You believe everyone has the right to know the truth, and you are vigilant in communicating that.

Work it

You are powerful because you are:

- Direct
- Well-informed
- Constructive
- A believer in integrity above all else
- Transparent

Own it

Get inspired by these kindred brands:

Soledad O'Brien - Brene Brown

Bring it

Amplify your strengths:

- Don't be afraid to give a bad review in the spirit of education; just be sure to also provide recommendations or solutions grounded in your expertise.

HOLLAH!

Bonus: What's your Why?
Find the worksheet at:
orangeandbergamot.com/bonus

Your Brand Mix Mastery:

 MAVEN x BFF

the sage.

You're the one people go to for comfort and wisdom. No matter the situation, you're always able to offer guidance — but out of tact, you only offer it to those who ask.

Work it

You are powerful because you are:

- Insightful
- Peacemaking
- Honest
- Sensible
- Always there for others

Own it

Get inspired by these kindred brands:

Gandhi - Stanford University

Bring it

Amplify your strengths:

- When giving advice, use relevant examples from your own experience and break down how you were able to handle a particular situation.

MAVEN
x BFF

Your Brand Mix Mastery:

 MAVEN x GEM

the mentor.

You have the strength, expertise, and control people seek when they need guidance; however, you're also sensitive and caring enough to make people comfortable, even at their most vulnerable.

Work it

You are powerful because you are:

- Passionate about helping others through guidance
- Willing to share your moments of vulnerability in order to set positive examples
- Emotionally intelligent
- Able to see the best in people

Own it

Get inspired by these kindred brands:

Oprah Winfrey - John Wooden

Bring it

Amplify your strengths:

- You are most effective with your skillset when you can have direct contact with your audience; seek out speaking and one-on-one opportunities.

Your Brand Mix Mastery:

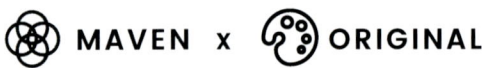 MAVEN x ORIGINAL

the luminary.

Your main purpose is to enlighten others, and your artistic side helps you do so in creative ways. People look to you for inspiration and motivation, and you enjoy empowering others through what you uniquely have to offer.

Work it

You are powerful because you are:

- Creative
- Great at explaining new concepts to others
- Passionate
- Known expert in a specific area
- Spirited

Own it

Get inspired by these kindred brands:

The Getty - GOOP

Bring it

Amplify your strengths:

- You are seen as a curator of ideas by others; jot down creative ways you can share your knowledge through your unique viewpoint, perhaps utilizing new media or direct experiences.

Your Brand Mix Mastery:

the tutor.

You're always surprising people — your humility prevents you from letting on that you have a lot of cool stuff to share. You may actually know it all, but you never come across as a know-it-all, instead being engaging and approachable.

Work it

You are powerful because you are:

- Humble
- Knowledgeable
- Good at simplifying material for others
- Fun
- Articulate

Own it

Get inspired by these kindred brands:

HGTV - Marie Forleo

Bring it

Amplify your strengths:

- Use a healthy dose of humor to be relatable and break down potential barriers someone might have to learning something new.

MAVEN
x Charismatic

IRL INFLUENCE*HER*

Lauren Messiah

Founder, The School of Style
@laurenmessiah

Photo credit: Anthony Naylor, Visions Entertainment Group

WHY WE THINK LAUREN IS A PERFECT MAVEN:
Lauren is driven by a desire to make positive, lasting change in her client's lives by empowering them to own their strengths and be who they are. She takes her expertise in her field and evolves with technology to share her knowledge — currently, virtual sessions, private Facebook groups, email newsletters, YouTube tutorials (and we're sure, a TV show soon enough!). Learn from her at laurenmessiah.com.

What makes you excited about your work?
Seeing my clients transform from the outside in fuels me. I love creating content that makes a lasting change in women's lives. Whether it's putting together a style series on YouTube or creating a 10-day style challenge that is the catalyst for change far beyond style, it feels amazing knowing that what I do truly makes a difference.

Can you share any struggles and how you've overcome them?
My biggest struggle has been confidence and owning my worth, which probably explains the mission behind my work — helping women overcome those same obstacles through the power of style. Overcoming confidence issues is a lifelong journey, but I am big on self help and deep inner work, and I definitely infuse that knowledge into my work as a stylist. My clients come in for a new dress and leave with a new outlook on life. Tricked them ;)

Who is your muse?
Oprah, Howard Stern, and Rihanna (couldn't pick just one) because they have all built an empire based on being completely true to themselves, and each make an impact in a very unique way. PS- If you haven't listened to the podcast *Making Oprah*, listen to it now!

What's next for you?
My mission in life is to change the way women get dressed — so expanding my reach is next for me. That means more speaking engagements and a television show.

Words to live by:

"Remember, it's ok to get what you want from life." Stuart Wilde

"I like to learn. That's an art and a science." Katherine Johnson

contemplative

ATTENTIVE

Insightful

intelligent

wise

Channel your inner:

Ruth Bader Ginsburg

MAJOR ARCHETYPE

the brilliant

2

You are all about acquiring and spreading knowledge. You love information and facts — finding them, gathering them, sticking to them. In fact (pun intended), you're a genius of sorts; you can never learn enough. Although some may see you as the nerdy type, you know you use your intellect in powerful ways.

X MAVEN	=	Philosopher
X GAMECHANGER	=	Genius
X IDEALIST	=	Thinker
X EXPLORER	=	Scholar
X POWERHOUSE	=	Egalitarian
X BOSS	=	Prodigy
X BRILLIANT	=	Academic
X REBEL	=	Whiz
X BFF	=	Realist
X GEM	=	Allocator
X ORIGINAL	=	Poet
X CHARISMATIC	=	Geek

Your Brand Mix Mastery:

 **BRILLIANT x MAVEN**

the philosopher.

You love to question everything, and understand that there is often more than meets the eye to the so-called "straight forward" aspects of life. One might say you're "enlightened," and you enjoy sharing your studies with the world.

Work it

You are powerful because you are:

- Investigative
- Knowledgeable
- Creative
- Passionate about learning
- A proponent of learning and education

Own it

Get inspired by these kindred brands:

Martha Nussbaum - Eckhart Tolle

Bring it

Amplify your strengths:

- Because your studies are often in-depth and high-level, be sure to connect with real people through conversations, get feedback. It will make your work that much more relevant and impactful.

Your Brand Mix Mastery:

👓 BRILLIANT x ⬢ GAMECHANGER

the genius.

You're devoted, always thinking of the next step. You love to be the one who is able to solve problems of today, but also prepared to solve potential problems in the future.

Work it

You are powerful because you are:

- Always in productive thought
- Focused
- Known for a strong work ethic
- Intelligent
- A problem solver

Own it

Get inspired by these kindred brands:

Katherine Johnson - Stephen Hawking

Bring it

Amplify your strengths:

- You may find that others are sometimes wary because you are always one step ahead. Be transparent with your process so that they can better understand how you got there.

Your Brand Mix Mastery:

 BRILLIANT x IDEALIST

the thinker.

Your brain doesn't have a "power off" button, but you find that this gets you ahead. Your ability to analyze every situation with empathy is what sets you apart from the rest.

Work it

You are powerful because you are:
- Inquisitive
- Analytical
- Empathetic
- Tactful
- Thoughtful

Own it

Get inspired by these kindred brands:

Angela Merkel - Amal Clooney

Bring it

Amplify your strengths:
- You are skilled at taking what you know and using that to empower others in a positive way. Get your ideas out there through speeches, articles, social media, volunteer work. Be vocal.

BRILLIANT
x Idealist

Your Brand Mix Mastery:

 BRILLIANT x EXPLORER

the scholar.

You are a lover of details, and enjoy completing daunting tasks. You are always seeking answers — challenges are fun and exciting.

Work it

You are powerful because you are:

- Curious
- Independent
- Self-guided
- Tactful
- Full of energy

Own it

Get inspired by these kindred brands:

Babbel - Eyewitness Travel Guides

Bring it

Amplify your strengths:

- You know you wouldn't make recommendations if it wasn't rooted in research. Provide comfort for those who may be hesitant about exploring something new by displaying it.

Your Brand Mix Mastery:

👓 **BRILLIANT** x ⚡ **POWERHOUSE**

the egalitarian.

You understand that everyone should be treated fairly and that there is a place for everyone; but you're also strong enough to stand up for yourself when you deserve something greater than what you already have.

Work it

You are powerful because you are:

- Bright
- Fair
- Sympathetic to others' experiences
- Helpful
- Great at making decisions

Own it

Get inspired by these kindred brands:

Ruth Bader Ginsberg - *The New York Times*

Bring it

Amplify your strengths:

- You use your intellect for impact. Others follow because of your confidence and commitment to your values. Put them out there and they'll be galvanized.

BRILLIANT
x Powerhouse

HOLLAH!

Bonus: Align with your Tribe
Find the how-to at:
orangeandbergamot.com/bonus

Your Brand Mix Mastery:

 BRILLIANT x BOSS

the prodigy.

You're smart as a whip without coming across as a know-it-all, and you have the confidence to match. You're all about achieving short-term and long-term goals, no matter what it takes.

Work it

You are powerful because you are:
- Motivated
- Clever
- Accomplished
- Thorough with every task
- Self-assured

Own it

Get inspired by these kindred brands:

Kamala Harris - Priyanka Joshi

Bring it

Amplify your strengths:
- You've worked hard to get where you are. Although you're not one to flaunt, inspire others by opening up about your journey, including the struggles and how you overcame them.

Your Brand Mix Mastery:

👓 **BRILLIANT** x 👓 **BRILLIANT**

the academic.

Your brand is 100 percent Brilliant. There's nothing you love more than the pursuit of knowledge . . . except maybe talking about what you've learned. People come to you for information on a variety of topics.

Work it

You are powerful because you are:

- Scholarly
- Knowledgeable
- Willing to challenge the status quo for discovery
- Passionate about sharing information
- A proponent of learning and education

Own it

Get inspired by these kindred brands:

Scholastic – Jennifer Doudna

Bring it

Amplify your strengths:

- You've amassed an enormous amount of knowledge; but that doesn't always equal wisdom. Be sure to get your nose out of a book and into the real world to appreciate its potential impact.

👓 **BRILLIANT**
x Brilliant

Your Brand Mix Mastery:

👓 **BRILLIANT** x ✺ **REBEL**

the whiz.

You may be a bit of a nerd, but you have an "edgy" side as well; you're free-thinking and highly independent. You tend to put your personal and professional values above the status quo.

Work it

You are powerful because you are:

- One to do what you like, not what others expect
- Witty
- Bold
- Self-assured
- Productive alone and in partnerships or teams

Own it

Get inspired by these kindred brands:

Washington Post - Rachel Maddow

Bring it

Amplify your strengths:

- You see what others don't. People admire your ability to ask the right questions, based on the information you've gathered. The dfference is you're willing to go the extra mile to get answers. Stay curious.

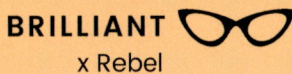

BRILLIANT 👓
x Rebel

Your Brand Mix Mastery:

the realist.

You're studious and attentive, and every move you make is done with a specific goal in mind. Because you "stick to the facts" without judgement, people have come to trust your recommendations.

Work it

You are powerful because you are:

- Practical
- Keep the "big picture" in mind
- A friendly face
- Independent
- Traditional

Own it

Get inspired by these kindred brands:

Sally Yates - *The Economist*

Bring it

Amplify your strengths:

- People find you reliable and comforting in that your work is consistent and without any frills. Keep emotion out of it to continue to deserve that trust.

Your Brand Mix Mastery:

 BRILLIANT x GEM

the allocator.

You may be a bit of a smarty pants, but it's all founded in love for other people (and the planet). You enjoy taking the resources you have or know of and helping them become attainable for those who need them.

Work it

You are powerful because you are:
- Friendly
- Warm-hearted
- Always thinking of others
- Clever
- Grateful

Own it

Get inspired by these kindred brands:

PBS - World Wildlife Fund

Bring it

Amplify your strengths:
- You're a bleeding heart but with the knowledge to back you up. Empower others with easy-to-understand, sharable information so that they can take up your cause as well (infographics, stats on social media, etc.)

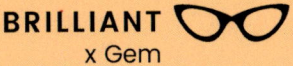

Your Brand Mix Mastery:

 BRILLIANT x ORIGINAL

the poet.

You believe in the power of words, and know how to use them to heal people or inspire them. You continually care for others and always aim to do the right thing.

Work it — You are powerful because you are:

- Analytical
- Creative
- Thoughtful
- Empathetic
- Adventurous

Own it — Get inspired by these kindred brands:

Paolo Cuelho - Margaret Atwood

Bring it — Amplify your strengths:

- You know the power of the pen (and the creative mind). Get it documented where you can ensure everlasting effect: novels, online, pull quotes, social media. Produce.

BRILLIANT
x Original

Your Brand Mix Mastery:

👓 **BRILLIANT** x ☀ **CHARISMATIC**

the geek.

Your personality is smart, witty, and a little bit dorky—and you're all the more lovable because of it. People admire your attentiveness to detail and the way you remember things that matter.

Work it

You are powerful because you are:

- Funny
- Intelligent
- Pondering
- Clever
- Happy-go-lucky

Own it

Get inspired by these kindred brands:

Stephen Colbert - Merriam-Webster (Twitter)

Bring it

Amplify your strengths:

- Your quick wit sets you apart. Use it for good by staying current on important events and provide a fresh perspective in that moment.

BRILLIANT 👓
x Charismatic

IRL INFLUENCE*HER*

Ashley Merrill

Founder, Lunya
@lunyaco

Photo credit: Hylah Hedgepeth

WHY WE THINK ASHLEY IS A PERFECT BRILLIANT:

Ashley quite literally loses sleep if she hasn't been able to solve a problem. Taking her intellect, education, and a step-by-step approach, she put in the hard work to solve sleepwear for the modern woman. This drive to problem solve has also led her to be an advocate for young women's education through her support of Girls Inc. and the funding of a new school for girls. lunya.co

What makes you excited about your work?
I feel so confident in our product and the team we have that I'm constantly excited. Hitting new goals, executing new ideas and innovations with a team is exhilarating. I love the challenge in my work; I'm never bored and always learning. Building a company isn't a mountain you summit, it's an ongoing series of rolling hills that keep you always guessing and pushing your boundaries.

Can you share any struggles and how you've overcome them?
People leadership can be emotionally exhausting. I care a lot about people and when I run into walls with employees I stay up all night for days on end grappling with what to do. I'm working on not having it affect me so much.

Who is your muse?
When I think about people I'm inspired by I would say my husband because he takes this "can do" thing to the next level, Gloria Steinem for her unflinching passion and commitment to change, and Nancy Aossey for her lifetime of commitment to those in crisis.

What's next for you?
Lunya is growing by leaps and bounds so we're hiring a lot of new people and opening some new Bedrooms for people to experience our product in person. Lots of product development and exciting innovation to come!

Words to live by:

"Be the change you wish to see in the world." Gandhi

This guides a lot of my ambitions. It's easy to look around you and find problems but it's powerful to realize you can have a hand in making things better.

> "I had to create an equivalent for what I felt about what I was looking at — not copy it."
>
> Georgia O'Keefe

Creative

unique

introspective

observant

INVENTIVE

Channel your inner:

Diane von Furstenberg

MAJOR ARCHETYPE

the original

3

You find inspiration everywhere you go. What's more, you inspire others with the things you create. You love to build and design new things, and everything you touch carries a bit of personality and pizazz.

x Maven	=	Curator
x Gamechanger	=	Creator
x Idealist	=	Ponderer
x Explorer	=	Novelist
x Powerhouse	=	Celestial
x Boss	=	Composer
x Brilliant	=	Architect
x Rebel	=	Rule-breaker
x BFF	=	Classicist
x Gem	=	Affectionate
x Original	=	Virtuoso
x Charismatic	=	Playful

Your Brand Mix Mastery:

 ORIGINAL x MAVEN

the curator.

You believe nothing goes without meaning, and everything — whether tangible or abstract — should be able to teach some type of lesson. You strive to educate others through the things you create.

Work it

You are powerful because you are:

- Thoughtful
- One to think outside the box
- Prolific
- In touch with people's emotions
- Inspired

Own it

Get inspired by these kindred brands:

PORTER - Diane von Furstenberg

Bring it

Amplify your strengths:

- You don't mind sharing what you've learned in order to help others find their own creativity. Empower people by being open, vocal and honest.

ORIGINAL
x Maven

Your Brand Mix Mastery:

the creator.

You feel true joy when you realize you've created something completey new and innovative. You're always looking for opportunities to flex your creative muscle or make something that will change the world.

Work it

You are powerful because you are:

- Educated
- Progressive
- Eager for a challenge
- Committed
- Inventive

Own it

Get inspired by these kindred brands:

Dua Lipa - Alexander McQueen

Bring it

Amplify your strengths:

- Make a bigger splash by focusing on one aspect and magnifying it in a bold way. Be a bit theatrical. Take risks to stand out from the competition.

ORIGINAL
x Gamechanger

Your Brand Mix Mastery:

 ORIGINAL x IDEALIST

the ponderer.

You love to explore all possibilities, personal and professional, whether in your head or in a tangible way. You live your life without regrets — because, of course, it's better than wondering what could have been.

Work it

You are powerful because you are:

- Dreamy
- Sanguine
- Inspiring
- One to work well with others
- Appreciative and promote luxury

Own it

Get inspired by these kindred brands:

Museum of Ice Cream - Dreamworks

Bring it

Amplify your strengths:

- Look for the beauty in everything. This is how you find inspiration — which is how you can continue to inspire others.

ORIGINAL
x Idealist

Your Brand Mix Mastery:

 ORIGINAL x EXPLORER

the novelist.

You love to express your creative side, and often get lost in daydreams. You aren't afraid to take risks, and it is important for you to feel understood.

Work it

You are powerful because you are:

- Creative
- The life of the party
- Known for a strong work ethic
- A great navigator
- Humble

Own it

Get inspired by these kindred brands:

Georgia O'Keefe - Elizabeth Gilbert

Bring it

Amplify your strengths:

- Provide opportunities for your audience to have an experience with you through writing, art, speaking or showing them something they may not have seen before.

Your Brand Mix Mastery:

ORIGINAL x POWERHOUSE

the celestial.

Your confidence in your creativity pulls others into your orbit. You are strong-willed and aren't afraid of a challenge; in fact, you think they're fun.

Work it

You are powerful because you are:

- Individualistic
- Unique
- Strong
- Intelligent
- Proud without being cocky

Own it

Get inspired by these kindred brands:

Versace - Carine Roitfeld

Bring it

Amplify your strengths:

- Put your ideas out there and without flinching. Your confidence in your creative abilities pulls others into your orbit, without you even trying.

ORIGINAL
x Powerhouse

Your Brand Mix Mastery:

ORIGINAL x BOSS

the composer.

You know what you want, and you go for it. There's no doubt you put everything you've got into what you produce. People are loyal to you because you hold such high standards for yourself and what you create.

Work it

You are powerful because you are:

- Creative
- Persistent
- Strong
- Tactful
- Quality-driven

Own it

Get inspired by these kindred brands:

Kelly Wearstler - Rihanna

Bring it

Amplify your strengths:

- Show others why an artistically-created product is far better than thoughtless one. Share your process to get there.

ORIGINAL
x Boss

Your Brand Mix Mastery:

 ORIGINAL x BRILLIANT

the architect.

You are always looking at things from a unique angle. You understand that everything has to start somewhere — so you're rarely afraid to take a plunge.

Work it

You are powerful because you are:

- Creative
- Open-minded
- A good listener
- Thoughtful
- Always striving to improve

Own it

Get inspired by these kindred brands:

Albert Einstein - Simone de Beauvoir

Bring it

Amplify your strengths:

- You are methodical in your creativity; best to rely on well-thought out ideas than abstract ones. Your audience will appreciate it.

ORIGINAL
x Brilliant

Your Brand Mix Mastery:

 ORIGINAL x REBEL

the rule-breaker.

You know that you have to think outside the box to get the results you want, and you're not afraid to be unconventional. You value your vibrancy and confidence under the spotlight — often, despite conventions others may hold.

Work it

You are powerful because you are:
- Bold
- Honest
- Tactful
- Unique
- Free-thinking

Own it

Get inspired by these kindred brands:
Annie Leibovitz - Katy Perry

Bring it

Amplify your strengths:
- Let some vulnerability in to give the most life to your ideas. You inspire others with what you do with it, and often, in spite of it.

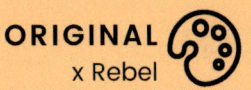

ORIGINAL
x Rebel

Your Brand Mix Mastery:

 ORIGINAL x BFF

the classicist.

The things you create are timeless. You'd rather provide a product or service that will last through the ages over one that is trendy or daring.

Work it

You are powerful because you are:

- Straightforward
- Non-wasteful
- Prefer comforting simplicity
- Create things that speak universally
- Enduring

Own it

Get inspired by these kindred brands:

Aerin Lauder - Restoration Hardware

Bring it

Amplify your strengths:

- Build confidence with your audience by showing your unique eye for quality. Point out details they may have missed, and include certifications to increase trust.

Your Brand Mix Mastery:

 ORIGINAL x GEM

the affectionate.

You are caring and unique in that you help people and solve problems in a snap. Your enjoy using your creativity for the benefit of others. You put your heart and soul into everything you do, and it shows.

Work it

You are powerful because you are:

- Caring
- Helpful
- Creative
- Hopeful
- Have faith in others

Own it

Get inspired by these kindred brands:

India Hicks - Etsy

Bring it

Amplify your strengths:

- Show your support of fostering others' creativity by providing opportunities for them to safely explore and experiment, online or in-person.

HOLLAH!
Bonus: Top 20 Touchpoints
Find the list at:
orangeandbergamot.com/bonus

Your Brand Mix Mastery:

 ORIGINAL x ORIGINAL

the virtuoso.

Your brand is 100 percent Original at heart. There's nothing you love more than to make things that speak to people and express who you truly are. Others love your creativity, honesty, and vision.

Work it

You are powerful because you are:

- Prolific
- Unique
- Like to try new things
- Able to convey ideas through art
- Imaginative

Own it

Get inspired by these kindred brands:

Sia - Art Basel

Bring it

Amplify your strengths:

- Your power is in your production: you create, create, create. Align yourself with an ally who can help you curate what you put out there to keep people curious about your work.

ORIGINAL
x Original

Your Brand Mix Mastery:

the playful.

Who said you have to be serious to have people take you seriously? Your rosy demeanor draws people to you, where they notice your originality and attentiveness to detail. You can't help yourself in being positive in everything you put out there. You're peachy keen.

Work it

You are powerful because you are:

- Sweet
- Playful
- Imaginative
- Curated
- Colorful

Own it

Get inspired by these kindred brands:

Bergdorf Goodman - Benefit Cosmetics

Bring it

Amplify your strengths:

- Get creative about ways you can engage your audience through events, VIP programs, wish lists, giveaways, little bonuses — ways that allow them to explore, curate and just feel good through your brand.

ORIGINAL
x Charismatic

IRL INFLUENCE*HER*

Christine Dovey

Owner and Principal Designer,
Christine Dovey Style Ltd.,
Iris and Ophelia
@christinedovey
@irisandophelia

Photo credit: Kayla Rocca

WHY WE THINK CHRISTINE IS A PERFECT ORIGINAL:

Like a true tastemaker, Christine doesn't set out to do so; it comes naturally with her pursuit of beauty through creativity and curation. She's an artist for art's sake and never short on a flow of ideas. She sets herself apart by owning her style, being comfortable in her uniqueness and working hard to put it out there — and why she's one of Canada's fave tastemakers. Get inspired: christinedovey.com

What makes you excited about your work?
The creative process is what always drives me in work, whether it's with my design or wellness business. I love creating things that feel artistic and editorial….and definitely strive to design rooms and/or content that have a sense of theatricality, like telling a story.

Can you share any struggles and how you've overcome them?
I am someone who loves ideas and creativity…likes dreaming up a million fantastical things that I one day hope to create and accomplish. Being a mom of four kids, it's sometimes hard to think that outlandish things are possible. I've recently started doing daily affirmations and am amazed by how much does come true when I simply choose to breathe life into it. When the steps for getting from A to B seem overwhelming, I've learned if I just choose to believe it and take one step towards my goals each and every day, I can make it happen.

Who is your muse?
Kelly Wearstler…because she is so unapologetically herself. KW's work is instantly recognizable as hers because she chose from the start, to not try and walk in the path of someone else but rather, to shout her truths from the rooftops. I adore her work for its amazing creativity and spirit. It oozes grit, passion and tenacity.

What's next for you?
I'm creating a book that mixes fictional fantasy with design, I am working on a super exciting new project called Cordial House, and we've recently purchased a property in my favourite place on earth, PEI — my dream is to have a whole bunch of different places I can transform into offbeat, cool design-centric properties that people can rent and enjoy. And finally, I'm continuing work on my wellness branch *Iris + Ophelia*, developing content that showcases how design and natural-based products can merge into something beautiful, and I've started to create some of my own product lines. An exciting product partnership is launching next spring…very excited about that!

Words to live by:

"We all have the power within us to create infinite magic…to put things out into the world we didn't even know we were capable of creating."

> "Nothing is impossible. The word itself says 'I'm possible!'" — Audrey Hepburn

Kind-Hearted

positive

ROMANTIC

Sensitve

Respectful

Channel your inner:

Emma Watson

MAJOR ARCHETYPE

♡ the idealist

4

You believe in and strive to represent the best in people. You're great at identifying just what people need and giving it to them with impeccable timing. Everything you do is performed with taste and care. People value your ability to relate emotionally not as an inconvenience, but as a virtue.

X MAVEN	=	Utopian
X GAMECHANGER	=	Optimist
X IDEALIST	=	Lover
X EXPLORER	=	Seeker
X POWERHOUSE	=	Gladiator
X BOSS	=	Elegant
X BRILLIANT	=	Fox
X REBEL	=	Paramour
X BFF	=	Romantic
X GEM	=	Passionate
X ORIGINAL	=	Muse
X CHARISMATIC	=	Whimsical

Your Brand Mix Mastery:

 IDEALIST x MAVEN

the utopian.

In your head is a picture of your ideal world, but you know you have to take steps to get to it. As a result, you are committed to helping others learn how they can improve the world around them, for the better good of all.

Work it

You are powerful because you are:

- Devoted to instructing others
- Patient
- Have others' best interest in mind
- Optimistic
- Kind

Own it

Get inspired by these kindred brands:

Melinda Gates - Hamdi Ulukaya

Bring it

Amplify your strengths:

- Identify specific ways in which individuals can contribute to larger issues; make it relatable and tangible so that they can see their positive impact.

IDEALIST
x Maven

Your Brand Mix Mastery:

♡ **IDEALIST** x ⬢ **GAMECHANGER**

the optimist.

Your outlook on life and the future may be a bit dreamy, but you've proven yourself capable of making even your wildest fantasies into reality. Your ideas always have a touch of optimism, and your belief in them inspires others.

Work it

You are powerful because you are:

- Positive
- Imaginative
- Productive
- Sensitive
- Artistic

Own it

Get inspired by these kindred brands:

PIXAR - Guillermo del Toro

Bring it

Amplify your strengths:

- Take quick notes on your phone or in a journal to document your ideas, even if they're not fully formed. Consider sharing your notes with someone who can you help you organize them and bring them out of your head and into reality.

IDEALIST ♡
x Gamechanger

Your Brand Mix Mastery:

 IDEALIST x IDEALIST

the lover.

Your brand is 100 percent Idealist at heart. You're dreamy, sensitive, and sweet all at once — but don't let people mistake that for softness. Your aspirations are ones you're determined to achieve, and you won't stop at anything until you're there.

Work it

You are powerful because you are:

- Considerate
- Thoughtful
- Determined
- Kind-hearted
- Gentle

Own it

Get inspired by these kindred brands:

Petra Nemcova - Victoria's Secret PINK

Bring it

Amplify your strengths:

- Although others may see your steadfast faith in goodness as naive, you know it is your choice to continue to do so; that is your power in a world full of doubt and fear. Own it and spread your light!

Your Brand Mix Mastery:

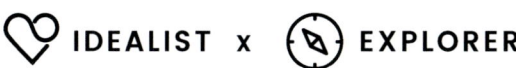 IDEALIST x EXPLORER

the seeker.

You approach the world with your arms, eyes, and heart wide open. What you know of the world, you love; and you love to discover things you don't already know. You don't claim to have all the answers, but that's part of the fun.

Work it

You are powerful because you are:

- Hopeful
- Curious
- Sincere
- Forthright
- Fun

Own it

Get inspired by these kindred brands:

Brooke Burke - Roxy

Bring it

Amplify your strengths:

- You inspire others through your positive outlook of your own experiences. Be open and share your journey; get descriptive and emotive in order for others to truly connect.

IDEALIST
x Explorer

Your Brand Mix Mastery:

♡ **IDEALIST** x ⚡ **POWERHOUSE**

the gladiator.

You may be known as a lover, but you'll fight for what you love. You aren't easily discouraged; instead, you keep going until you get what you want because of the strength in your beliefs.

Work it

You are powerful because you are:

- Determined
- Passionate
- Daring
- Able to inspire others through your actions
- Resilient

Own it

Get inspired by these kindred brands:

Wonder Woman - Olympics

Bring it

Amplify your strengths:

- Remember to balance your drive with your empathy. It's an important part of your pull to bring others along with you in your pursuit.

♡ **IDEALIST** x Powerhouse

HOLLAH!

Bonus: SEO 101
Find our top tips at:
orangeandbergamot.com/bonus

Your Brand Mix Mastery:

 IDEALIST x BOSS

the elegant.

You strive to bring out the very best in people and situations. You give everything you've got to ensure that whatever the task, you'll meet it with thoughfulness and attention to the highest detail, for the enjoyment of others.

Work it

You are powerful because you are:

- Quality-driven
- Positive
- Amicable
- Willing to go above and beyond for others
- Assured

Own it

Get inspired by these kindred brands:

Grace Kelly - American Girl Doll

Bring it

Amplify your strengths:

- Others look up to you because you seem to always have it all together, with a smile on your face. But you don't always have to be perfect; share your own "oops" moments to remain relatable.

IDEALIST x Boss

Your Brand Mix Mastery:

♡ **IDEALIST** x ◯◯ **BRILLIANT**

the fox.

You're perceptive and imaginative, yet sharp as a tack. It's about more than just being the beauty and the brains; it's also about being passionate about improving and contributing.

Work it

You are powerful because you are:

- Sensitive to others' emotional needs
- Enjoy studying or learning new things
- Recognized as an expert on a particular topic
- Witty
- Hopeful and optimistic about the future

Own it

Get inspired by these kindred brands:

Emma Watson - Girls Who Code

Bring it

Amplify your strengths:

- Sometimes passion comes across as irrational, so take the time to back up your claims with stats and figures you can use to further your cause.

♡ **IDEALIST**
x Brilliant

Your Brand Mix Mastery:

the paramour.

You're a lover with a catch — an unbeatable desire to conquer the status quo and create something of your own. Your passion makes you noticeably better at what you do.

Work it

You are powerful because you are:

- Daring
- Mysterious
- Independent
- Free-thinking
- Alluring

Own it

Get inspired by these kindred brands:

Bella Hadid - Revolve Clothing

Bring it

Amplify your strengths:

- Heighten your allure by not putting it all out there. Vet your communication to maintain a sense of mystery and curiosity about your brand. People will lose interest quickly if you don't leave anything to the imagination.

IDEALIST x Rebel

Your Brand Mix Mastery:

 IDEALIST x BFF

the romantic.

Your values are somewhat traditional yet sensual, and you love to add romantic details to the things you create. Others know they can rely on you to always be hopeful and optimistic.

Work it

You are powerful because you are:

- Consistently happy
- Appreciative of beauty both inside and out
- Open
- Sensitive to people's emotional needs
- Classic

Own it

Get inspired by these kindred brands:

Tiffany & Co - Ariana Grande

Bring it

Amplify your strengths:

- Express positivity in all your communication; your power lies in the ease of others to trust in your good-hearted nature, and they are attracted to you for that reason.

Your Brand Mix Mastery:

 IDEALIST x GEM

the passionate.

You're the epitome of love and support. Rather than viewing emotional sensitivity as a weakness, you see it as a strength. People love your passion and consideration for others.

Work it

You are powerful because you are:
- Warm-hearted
- Kind
- Love to take care of others
- Communicative
- Emotionally intelligent

Own it

Get inspired by these kindred brands:
Audrey Hepburn - Hallmark

Bring it

Amplify your strengths:
- Connect emotionally with others by using expressive language that conveys your uplifting spirit.

Your Brand Mix Mastery:

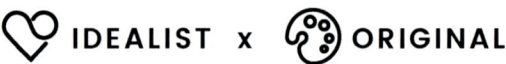 IDEALIST x ORIGINAL

the muse.

You carry inspiration wherever you go. You bring out the best in people by creating things that captivate them and make them feel good, allowing them to share the joy with those around them.

Work it

You are powerful because you are:

- Highly creative
- Thoughtful
- Inspired
- Emotionally intelligent
- Considerate

Own it

Get inspired by these kindred brands:

Disney - Miranda Kerr

Bring it

Amplify your strengths:

- In your process of creation, visualize how the end user would benefit from what you uniquely have to offer. Turn the tables and use that feeling as *your* muse.

IDEALIST
x Original

Your Brand Mix Mastery:

IDEALIST x CHARISMATIC

the whimsical.

You have a kind, light-hearted spirit that's easy to love. You enjoy inserting a touch of wit now and then to keep things sunny and fun.

Work it

You are powerful because you are:

- Hopeful
- Optimistic
- Fun-loving
- Make other people smile and laugh
- Uplifting

Own it

Get inspired by these kindred brands:

Bravo - tokidoki

Bring it

Amplify your strengths:

- Add a dose of delight by inserting little surprises once in a while (like a handwritten note, an extra sample or thoughtful gesture).

IDEALIST x Charismatic

IRL INFLUENCE*HER*

Zee Johnson

Founder, Wild Hearts PR
@zeejohnson

Photo credit: Jennifer Daigle

WHY WE THINK ZEE IS A PERFECT IDEALIST:
Zee has a certain "light" that attracts those around her to her (as is evidenced by her impressive client roster in just the first few months of her company!). She excels at communicating her positivity and passion both online and in person. Learn how she does it: instagram.com/ZeeJohnson

What makes you excited about your work?
I absolutely love knowing I played a part in growing someone's business. If they're not growing, I'm not growing so it excites me to find new and dynamic ways to help grow with my clients.

Can you share any struggles and how you've overcome them?
When I officially announced I was starting my own company and getting out of real estate, people had opinions about my lack of experience. Unlike when I was practicing real estate, I have real passion for the business I started which is reflected in the clients I currently have. I'm a huge believer if there's no passion behind your work, you're not doing the job to the best of your abilities.

Who is your muse?
I have many, but definitely Oprah! She overcame a lot in her rise to success but she never let it get in the way of her ambition and drive. I can relate heavily on going through a tremendous amount in my childhood, teen years and early adulthood, but I feel I've never let those struggles define me. Instead I put my energy into aspiring to inspire, and turning my dreams into reality regardless of judgement or obstacles.

What's next for you?
My company is currently focused on one niche that I'm passionate about, and I do well. I am expanding my company by bringing in other experts in different fields who are passionate about their own industries to run multiple divisions.

Words to live by:
"I used to have horrible cars, because I never had money, so I'd always end up broken down on the highway. When I stood there trying to flag someone down, nobody stopped. But when I pushed my own car, other drivers would get out and push with me.

If you want help, help yourself — people like to see that." Chris Rock

"**There are 360 degrees so why stick to one?**" Zaha Hadid

resilient

Passionate

Unconventional

Forward Thinking

INNOVATIVE

Channel your inner:

Whitney Wolfe Herd

MAJOR ARCHETYPE

the gamechanger 5

You are known for being ahead of your time, thinking outside the box and blazing a new path. You thrive off forward progress; in your opinion, anything can be improved with a little innovation. After all, why continue to do things the way they've always been done just because everyone else does that? Your mantra: be bold, be different.

X MAVEN	=	Groundbreaker
X GAMECHANGER	=	Trendsetter
X IDEALIST	=	Dreamer
X EXPLORER	=	Pathfinder
X POWERHOUSE	=	Influencer
X BOSS	=	Pioneer
X BRILLIANT	=	Strategist
X REBEL	=	Maverick
X BFF	=	Admired
X GEM	=	Philanthropist
X ORIGINAL	=	Avant-Garde
X CHARISMATIC	=	Visionary

Your Brand Mix Mastery:

 **GAMECHANGER x MAVEN**

the groundbreaker.

You believe that setting a good example is the best way to educate others. And what better way to set a good example than setting up a foundation for future success?

Work it

You are powerful because you are:

- Faithful
- Contemporary
- Driven to create things that are cutting-edge
- Forward-thinking
- Passionate about others' success

Own it

Get inspired by these kindred brands:

Katrina Lake - *Entrepreneur*

Bring it

Amplify your strengths:

- Because others want to learn from the example you set, take note of the ways in which you remain innovative. Be transparent and share them through steps, tips and advice.

Your Brand Mix Mastery:

 GAMECHANGER x

the trendsetter.

Your brand is 100 percent Gamechanger at heart. Your main goal is progress; why do things the way you've always done them when you could find cooler, faster ways that will dazzle the world? Your brand strives to break the mold and set the stage for the time to come.

Work it

You are powerful because you are:

- A modern and progressive mindset
- Highly productive
- Innovative
- Great at problem-solving
- High standards

Own it

Get inspired by these kindred brands:

Amazon - Elon Musk

Bring it

Amplify your strengths:

- Know that you don't need approval from others to experiment; they'll believe it when they see it. Keep going. Your mantra should be, "If you build it, they will come."

GAMECHANGER
x Gamechanger

Your Brand Mix Mastery:

 **GAMECHANGER x IDEALIST**

the dreamer.

You're always dreaming about what you'd like to introduce to the world next. The past is of no consequence to you; that's done and done, and you like to focus on the future and how you can maximize benefit to the world.

Work it

You are powerful because you are:

- Ambitious
- Inventive
- Enthusiastic
- Optimistic
- Devoted

Own it

Get inspired by these kindred brands:

The Boring Company - Virgin Airlines

Bring it

Amplify your strengths:

- You know at your core the value in what you are doing. When you stumble, see it as an opportunity for growth and be communicative about the positives toward the larger goal.

Your Brand Mix Mastery:

 GAMECHANGER x  **EXPLORER**

the pathfinder.

You love to make discoveries, because for everything new you find, you can make your creations that much more innovative. You strive to stay ahead of the game by exploring new avenues.

Work it

You are powerful because you are:
- Experimentational
- Creative
- Research-oriented
- Curious
- One to try new things to see the effects

Own it

Get inspired by these kindred brands:

SpaceX - Google

Bring it

Amplify your strengths:
- Help others understand what they might feel is scary and off-the-wall by taking them behind the scenes so they can share in your journey.

Your Brand Mix Mastery:

 GAMECHANGER x POWERHOUSE

the influencer.

You often find yourself leading the way — particularly when it comes to creating or selling brand-new ideas. Others admire your ability to think outside the box and set a good example for others by simply doing what you set out to do.

Work it

You are powerful because you are:
- Brilliant
- Charming
- Innovative
- Tough
- Thoughtful

Own it

Get inspired by these kindred brands:

Glossier - Sophia Amoruso

Bring it

Amplify your strengths:
- You have no problem blazing your own new path but tend to inadvertently leave others behind. Don't forget to be vocal about your accomplishments and milestones along the way — they inspire others by giving them something tangible to strive for.

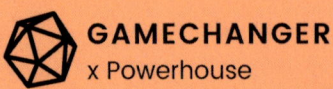

Your Brand Mix Mastery:

 GAMECHANGER x BOSS

the pioneer.

You have incredibly high standards for yourself, your team, and your commodity. You've got big goals and big ideas — the things you create are designed to change the world, for today and tomorrow.

Work it

You are powerful because you are:

- Able to predict future market needs and desires
- Creative
- Unwavering
- Willing to think outside of the box
- Resilient

Own it

Get inspired by these kindred brands:

Emily Weiss - Jeff Bezos

Bring it

Amplify your strengths:

- Your ideas and methods may not be for everyone and that's ok. Stay true to your goals but practice patience with those who can help you achieve them.

Your Brand Mix Mastery:

 GAMECHANGER x BRILLIANT

the strategist.

You're always working toward some sort of goal, and you do so in a sensible, meticulous way. Rather than focusing on the past, you like to think about what you can accomplish in the future.

Work it

You are powerful because you are:

- Hard-working
- Detail-oriented
- Conscious of all angles before acting
- Clever
- Perfectionist mentality

Own it

Get inspired by these kindred brands:

Whitney Wolfe Herd - Tesla

Bring it

Amplify your strengths:

- Make sure your product or service isn't just shiny, but practical. Ask your core audience if you're meeting their existing needs, and ask what their pain points are to meet future needs.

Your Brand Mix Mastery:

the maverick.

You aren't afraid to stray from the status quo if it means creating something new and groundbreaking. You often find yourself setting the standard for others in your industry by recognizing what isn't working and fixing it.

Work it

You are powerful because you are:

- Risktaking
- Independent
- Adventurous
- Self-driven
- Contemporary

Own it

Get inspired by these kindred brands:

Sara Blakely -   Sir Richard Branson

Bring it

Amplify your strengths:

- Do an audit of your competitors and take note of opportunities for improvement. You don't need to "name names," but instead, focus on what you're doing differently (and not just who may not be doing it right).

Your Brand Mix Mastery:

 **GAMECHANGER x BFF**

the admired.

Though you're a bit of a traditionalist, you're also able to carefully predict trends and adjust your value accordingly. You like to provide what people are comfortable with while still managing to set yourself apart by thinking ahead.

Work it

You are powerful because you are:

- Trustworthy
- Able to predict future needs and desires
- Comforting
- Good at exercising forethought
- Consistent

Own it

Get inspired by these kindred brands:

Target - Kendra Scott

Bring it

Amplify your strengths:

- Stay ahead of the game by keeping up to date with what's happening in your industry. Take note of the ups and downs, and be honest and transparent about both in order to build trust with your core audience.

Your Brand Mix Mastery:

 GAMECHANGER x GEM

the philanthropist.

You believe in forward progress that benefits not only yourself, but those who are less fortunate (and for the world at large). You're particularly great at getting people to believe in and support your mission by conveying your passion in your ideas.

Work it

You are powerful because you are:

- Creative
- Considerate
- Generous
- Progressive
- Loving

Own it

Get inspired by these kindred brands:

Thrive Market - TOMS

Bring it

Amplify your strengths:

- When sharing your ideas, be sure to communicate "why" you're doing what you're doing. It allows others to identify with their own desires for the future, and builds an emotional connection.

Your Brand Mix Mastery:

 **GAMECHANGER** x **ORIGINAL**

the avant-garde.

The things you create are thought-provoking, have an ingenious touch and always center on new ideas. Your main goal is to move your industry or society at large forward through what you uniquely produce.

Work it

You are powerful because you are:
- Inventive
- Progressive
- Pondering
- Resolute
- Visionary

Own it

Get inspired by these kindred brands:
Coco Chanel - Zaha Hadid

Bring it

Amplify your strengths:
- Your main asset is your forward-thinking originality. Be brave in it; don't shy away from how it sets you apart. You'll attract the right tribe.

Your Brand Mix Mastery:

 GAMECHANGER x CHARISMATIC

the visionary.

You spread your innovative ideas in a way that appeals to people's positive side, whether it's kindhearted, hopeful, or downright funny. You're all about using your inventiveness for good.

Work it

You are powerful because you are:

- Brilliant
- Charming
- Lighthearted
- Positive
- Unique

Own it

Get inspired by these kindred brands:

Airbnb - Snapchat

Bring it

Amplify your strengths:

- Get creative on how you can build connections through positive experiences with you and your brand. People crave engagement, relationships, meaning and a feeling of achievement.

HOLLAH!

Bonus: Social Media 101
Find our top tips at:
orangeandbergamot.com/bonus

IRL INFLUENCE*HER*

Anu Bhardwaj

Founder, Women INVESTING in Women DIGITAL, SHEQ, Qrypto Queens

Anu and her daughter, Arya

Photo credit: Alvaro Nates

WHY WE THINK ANU IS A PERFECT GAMECHANGER:

Anu is a bold, fearless leader who is driven by a purpose and who addresses today's needs with tomorrow's solutions. She doesn't get distracted by naysayers but rather, keeps her eye on the ball and doesn't hesitate to put her ideas out there and turn them into reality. Get inspired and join the other 1 million (and counting!) in her tribe: facebook.com/womeninvesting

What makes you excited about your work?
The ability to create change while creating my own destiny. I love innovating what's so needed in our world, especially when it comes to the economic empowerment of women.

Can you share any struggles and how you've overcome them?
There are always fires that need to be put out as an entrepreneur! It's amazing how far a dollar can stretch with enough creativity. Sometimes, I think I am a magician. My advice: It's super critical to be clear on what you are doing and why, and then everything will fall into place. Resilience and grit are KEYS to success. My greatest struggle has been moving across four continents, 80 countries, for the past 20 years, many foreign languages not so foreign anymore and many friends in far off places who are now extended family. This has actually turned into my greatest asset: a vast global network, a depth of experiences and cultures in a profound manner, and the ability to communicate across borders, effortlessly.

Who is your muse?
My daughter, Arya Sitara Bhardwaj, is my muse. She has boundless energy and creativity, and has THE BEST JOKES EVER. She is super sensitive and kind, and never hesitates to question what she doesn't understand. On top of that, she's fearless and open to new adventures with such an open mind and heart.

What's next for you?
I'll be launching SHEQ Wallets in partnership with Women INVESTING in Women DIGITAL, QRYPTO QUEENS, and The State of Women Institute in six continents around the globe later this year. SHEQ is the world's first multi-asset, multi-functional crypto wallet by women for women. Our global conference series "Blockchain on the Beach" will also be launching in November in Laguna Beach (learn more at qryptoqueens.com or thestateofwomen.com).

Words to live by:

"True happiness is found within."

> "You have to participate relentlessly in the manifestation of your own blessings." — Elizabeth Gilbert

enthusiastic

INQUISITIVE

Eager to experience new things

Highly Autonomous

individualistic

Channel your inner:

J.K. Rowling

MAJOR ARCHETYPE

# the explorer

6

You love to learn everything you can about the world around you. You approach life with an open heart and starry eyes, and everything you do is an adventure. People admire your upbeat, can-do attitude and conviction. Is there any challenge you won't take on?

x Maven	=	Scout
x Gamechanger	=	Inventor
x Idealist	=	Open Mind
x Explorer	=	Adventurer
x Powerhouse	=	Critic
x Boss	=	Climber
x Brilliant	=	Scientist
x Rebel	=	Inquisitor
x BFF	=	Inspector
x Gem	=	Conscientious
x Original	=	Animator
x Charismatic	=	Bright Spot

Your Brand Mix Mastery:

 EXPLORER x MAVEN

the scout.

You love making observations through thorough research or casual notations and sharing them with the world. The more you know, the stronger your brand is, and the better the world can be.

Work it You are powerful because you are:

- A lover of adventure
- Passionate about educating others
- Eager to try new things
- Constantly learning
- Easily adaptable to new circumstances

Own it Get inspired by these kindred brands:

Lonely Planet - Girl Scouts of USA

Bring it Amplify your strengths:

- In your communication, use open-ended questions that empower others to embark on their own journeys of discovery.

EXPLORER
x Maven

Your Brand Mix Mastery:

 EXPLORER x GAMECHANGER

the inventor.

When you make a discovery, you also make a connection — what reality would this revelation bring? How can you use your discovery to increase productivity or make the world a better place?

Work it

You are powerful because you are:

- Determined
- Resourceful
- Productive
- Progressive
- A lover of expanding understanding

Own it

Get inspired by these kindred brands:

NASA - KAYAK

Bring it

Amplify your strengths:

- Always ask yourself what you can do to improve your value, product or service. There should never be a dull moment in which you have zero progress.

EXPLORER
x Gamechanger

Your Brand Mix Mastery:

 EXPLORER x IDEALIST

the open mind.

You thrive on new discoveries, whether they're about your industry or just the world around you. Others admire your passion for learning and love for life.

Work it   You are powerful because you are:
- Inquisitive
- Upbeat
- Comfortable challenging own beliefs
- A vivid communicator
- Trusting

Own it   Get inspired by these kindred brands:

National Geographic - Elizabeth Gilbert

Bring it   Amplify your strengths:
- People look to you for your enthusiasm around embarking on new challenges. They may not have the courage to try something new and "fail" — show them the positives in every experience.

EXPLORER
x Idealist

Your Brand Mix Mastery:

 EXPLORER x EXPLORER

the adventurer.

Your brand is 100 percent Explorer at heart. You adore finding and learning about new things, then sharing them with the world. Nothing excites you more than an adventure, for the sake of adventure.

Work it

You are powerful because you are:

- Curious
- Active
- Never settled for anything less than the goal
- Hopeful
- Independent

Own it

Get inspired by these kindred brands:

REI - Laura Dekker

Bring it

Amplify your strengths:

- For you it's all about the journey, not the destination. You're a doer; take others along on your adventures via social media, photography, live videos, etc.

Your Brand Mix Mastery:

⊙ EXPLORER x ⚡ POWERHOUSE

the critic.

Your sense of authority makes you the perfect person to lead others into exploration. Others respect your experience and seek your advice, constructive criticism, and words of encouragement.

Work it

You are powerful because you are:

- Accomplished
- Great at taking charge
- Always know the right thing to say
- Supportive of others without coddling them
- Inquisitive

Own it

Get inspired by these kindred brands:

Patagonia - Meryl Streep

Bring it

Amplify your strengths:

- Rather than imposing how you'd approach a new challenge on others, lead by example. When asked for advice, use your own relevant experiences.

Your Brand Mix Mastery:

 **EXPLORER** x **BOSS**

the climber.

You're an adventure seeker with a specific purpose in mind. Making discoveries is the name of your game, and you're notably good at it. You don't waste time wandering around; instead, you identify what you want and go find it.

Work it

You are powerful because you are:

- Curious
- Analytical
- Ambitious
- Hopeful
- Detail-oriented

Own it

Get inspired by these kindred brands:

Range Rover - *Conde Nast Traveler*

Bring it

Amplify your strengths:

- You're all about being selective in your pursuits. Others are attracted to you because of this; be vocal about your goals during your quest to achieve them.

Your Brand Mix Mastery:

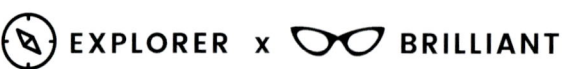 EXPLORER x BRILLIANT

the scientist.

You're motivated by facts, and research is one of your highest priorities. You strive to lead efforts that find, analyze, and share new information for the sake of educating.

Work it

You are powerful because you are:

- Focused on facts, not feelings
- Progressive
- Elite
- Research-focused
- Authoritative

Own it

Get inspired by these kindred brands:

Sally Ride - RAND Corporation

Bring it

Amplify your strengths:

- Although you are driven by the desire to discover (in detail), remember to share your discoveries with the average person via summarized reports, layman articles, press pieces. Your appeal will be tenfold.

Your Brand Mix Mastery:

 EXPLORER x REBEL

the inquisitor.

You're committed to seeing just where your passions will take you, even if it means being a little different. You don't mind standing out; in fact, you view your uniqueness as an advantage over those who tend to stick to the status quo.

Work it

You are powerful because you are:

- Resolute in ideas and goals
- Daring
- Bright
- Inquisitive
- Individualist

Own it

Get inspired by these kindred brands:

Anthony Bourdain - Jennifer Lawrence

Bring it

Amplify your strengths:

- You don't necessarily buy what others have said and done; you would rather find out for yourself. Keep asking the questions others wouldn't think to ask. Be their advocate.

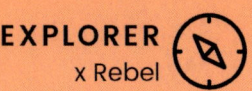
EXPLORER
x Rebel

Your Brand Mix Mastery:

 EXPLORER x BFF

the inspector.

You love to dive deep into the unknown, and you often go with your gut when it comes to making decisions. You stand by your veracity, and others know they can rely on your drive to seek the truth.

Work it

You are powerful because you are:

- Analytical
- Creative
- Trustworthy
- Known for a robust work ethic
- Handy

Own it

Get inspired by these kindred brands:

The North Face - Fodor's

Bring it

Amplify your strengths:

- Because people look to you for your opinions, attempt to answer all questions and comments that come your way. You stand out by being a reliable source of new information.

EXPLORER
x BFF

Your Brand Mix Mastery:

 **EXPLORER** x **GEM**

the **conscientious.**

You don't mind going out of your way to help others learn how to take care of other people (and the planet); in fact, you enjoy it. People admire your passion and selfless attitude.

Work it

You are powerful because you are:
- Confident
- Generous
- Altruistic
- Outgoing
- Comfortable sticking up for yourself and others

Own it

Get inspired by these kindred brands:

Jane Goodall - The Sierra Club

Bring it

Amplify your strengths:
- You attract others by taking action, not just talking about it. But start small in order to garner support and bring others along with you.

Your Brand Mix Mastery:

 **EXPLORER** x **ORIGINAL**

the animator.

You love to seek out fresh possibilities with the things you create. Others recognize you as a fearless artist who values new and different ideas, and the process to bring them forth.

Work it

You are powerful because you are:

- Creative
- A variety-seeker
- Willing to dig deep
- Individualistic
- Self-motivated

Own it

Get inspired by these kindred brands:

J.K. Rowling - Walt Disney

Bring it

Amplify your strengths:

- You are one who can easily visualize and get into the weeds of what you create. Keep a trusted circle of colleagues who can ensure you're not overcomplicating it for your audience, and who will hold you accountable with your deadlines.

EXPLORER
x Original

Your Brand Mix Mastery:

 EXPLORER x CHARISMATIC

the bright spot.

Due to your overall confidence, you don't mind being in the spotlight and putting what you got out there. You use your sense of humor to attract others who believe in your mission: to discover new ideas, then bring them to light.

Work it

You are powerful because you are:

- Bold
- Funny
- Bright
- Positive
- Curious

Own it

Get inspired by these kindred brands:

PopSugar - Trader Joe's

Bring it

Amplify your strengths:

- Keep it light; you have a lot to share and you can be confident in knowing that with a bit of humor, others will be open to exploring it with you.

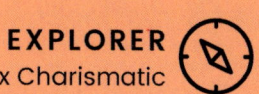

IRL INFLUENCE*HER*

Liz Arch

Founder, Primal Yoga
@lizarch

Photo credit: JQ Williams

WHY WE THINK LIZ IS A PERFECT EXPLORER:

Liz will be the first to tell you she's experienced a lot to get where she is today. She doesn't claim to have all the answers for everyone, but rather, uses her journey to inspire others to discover their own answers, along their own paths. Explore with her at lizarch.com

What makes you excited about your work?
I love empowering people with tools to help them step into their greatest strength, courage, confidence, resiliency and healing. The most impactful thing about what I do is that I don't really do anything; my students and clients are the ones who really do the work and I simply get to hold compassionate space to witness their transformation unfolding. It's far more powerful for me to empower people to be their own greatest teachers and healers rather than trying to be the one doing the healing.

Can you share any struggles and how you've overcome them?
I think the biggest obstacle I've had to overcome is simply getting out of my own way. I've been through a lot of trauma in my life and there were so many moments where I wanted to quit or make myself as small as possible because it felt safer to be small. Fear, self-doubt and anxiety have been my constant companions, but rather than giving into my fears, I make a conscious choice everyday to step into my courage. I remind myself that courage isn't the absence of fear, but the strength to move forward despite it.

Who is your muse?
I think we should all love ourselves enough to be our own muse! I've always felt so socially awkward and introverted around others, so my work has been to become truly comfortable in my own skin. When I step onto my yoga mat all my awkwardness seems to fall away and I feel truly graceful, powerful and present.

What's next for you?
I'm re-launching my website and debuting my new YouTube Channel and podcast. I'm also releasing my first book titled The Courage to Rise in January 2019, published by WilliamMorrow/HarperCollins.

Words to live by:

"Maybe the journey isn't so much about becoming anything. Maybe it's about unbecoming everything that isn't really you so you can be who you were meant to be in the first place."

"Ditch the dream and be a doer."
Shonda Rhimes

DRIVEN

Leader Mentality

independent

free-thinking

organized

Channel your inner:
Beyoncé

MAJOR ARCHETYPE

the powerhouse 7

You're not a sheep, you're a lion. You're bold and carry the type of confidence others wish they had. You have no problem taking charge in sticky situations; in fact, people value your leadership skills and frequently look to you for guidance.

X MAVEN	=	Coach
X GAMECHANGER	=	Crusader
X IDEALIST	=	Connector
X EXPLORER	=	Captain
X POWERHOUSE	=	Queen
X BOSS	=	Mogul
X BRILLIANT	=	Ambassador
X REBEL	=	Demagogue
X BFF	=	CEO
X GEM	=	Advocate
X ORIGINAL	=	Director
X CHARISMATIC	=	Charmer

Your Brand Mix Mastery:

⚡ **POWERHOUSE** x ✦ **MAVEN**

the coach.

People recognize you as someone experienced with great leadership abilities, and they seek out your wisdom whenever possible. You pride yourself on what you have to offer in terms of knowledge and empowerment.

Work it

You are powerful because you are:
- Encouraging
- Seasoned
- Enthusiastic
- Skilled in educating others in a motivating way
- Practical

Own it

Get inspired by these kindred brands:

Michelle Obama - *Glamour*

Bring it

Amplify your strengths:
- Swoop in and save the day when those around you are having a hard time. They'll remember your sense of responsibility and leadership.

⚡ **POWERHOUSE**
x Maven

Your Brand Mix Mastery:

⚡ **POWERHOUSE** x ⬢ **GAMECHANGER**

the crusader.

You're always thinking and powering ahead. People generally look up to you for inspiration, motivation, and advice for success. They know you've got your eye not only on the ball, but where it's headed too.

Work it

You are powerful because you are:

- Rarely satisfied
- Highly productive
- Intelligent
- Innovative
- Known to have great leadership skills

Own it

Get inspired by these kindred brands:

Apple - Arianna Huffington

Bring it

Amplify your strengths:

- You attract others by setting bold initiatives. People are inspired by your confidence; they want to follow your lead. It makes them feel bold too.

HOLLAH!

Bonus: Website 101
Find our top tips at:
orangeandbergamot.com/bonus

POWERHOUSE ⚡
x Gamechanger

Your Brand Mix Mastery:

⚡ **POWERHOUSE** x ♡ **IDEALIST**

the connector.

You may be known for your leadership and achievements, but it doesn't mean you don't have a soft and sensitive side. In fact, your emotional intelligence and dreams for the future are how you've surged ahead of the rest.

Work it

You are powerful because you are:

- Spirited
- Emotionally adept
- Hospitable
- Powerful
- Passionate

Own it

Get inspired by these kindred brands:

Pope Francis - Ava DuVernay

Bring it

Amplify your strengths:

- You are steadfast in believing the very best of those around you. Encourage that by never expecting less, and being vocal about it.

⚡ **POWERHOUSE**
x Idealist

Your Brand Mix Mastery:

⚡ POWERHOUSE x 🧭 EXPLORER

the captain.

You love adventure, and you always know which path is best to take. People come to you for guidance, and you provide a comforting and reliable lead.

Work it

You are powerful because you are:

- Intelligent
- A leader
- Trustworthy
- A risk-taker
- Insightful

Own it

Get inspired by these kindred brands:

Patty Jenkins - Marcus Lemonis

Bring it

Amplify your strengths:

- Your uniqueness lies in your power to seek out new discoveries and bring them to light; they want to be found. Create new ways to find them.

Your Brand Mix Mastery:

⚡ **POWERHOUSE** x ⚡ **POWERHOUSE**

the queen.

Your brand is 100 percent Powerhouse. You're known for getting things done and looking good while doing it. People like to put you in charge — and that's exactly where you like to be.

Work it

You are powerful because you are:

- Highly motivated
- Hardworking
- Strong
- Confident
- Bold

Own it

Get inspired by these kindred brands:

Beyoncé - Girlboss Media

Bring it

Amplify your strengths:

- You're a doer; you're not intimidated by a challenge and don't need permission to get it going. Take the lead — even if it's a small step — and you'll encourage others to do the same.

⚡ **POWERHOUSE**
x Powerhouse

Your Brand Mix Mastery:

⚡ **POWERHOUSE** x 🎯 **BOSS**

the mogul.

You're the BOSS everyone aspires to be: productive, admirable, and great at taking charge (and taking over when needed). Your leadership abilities are highly respected by people in and outside of your industry.

Work it

You are powerful because you are:

- Easily motivated
- One to thrive on productivity
- Good at prioritizing tasks
- Impactful
- "Get things done" attitude

Own it

Get inspired by these kindred brands:

Anna Wintour - Nike

Bring it

Amplify your strengths:

- You operate on high level of self-motivation. You inspire others with your eagerness to jump in and see it through. Your mantra should be, "Just do it. And do it right."

POWERHOUSE ⚡
x Boss

Your Brand Mix Mastery:

⚡ **POWERHOUSE** x 👓 **BRILLIANT**

the ambassador.

You bridge the gap between leadership and know-how. You're an immense value to your industry due to your expertise and people skills.

Work it

You are powerful because you are:

- Eager to both learn and share information with others
- Highly productive
- Good at leading and managing people
- Encourage others' growth

Own it

Get inspired by these kindred brands:

NPR - Christiane Amanpour

Bring it

Amplify your strengths:

- Much of your power lies in the amount of knowledge you've acquired. Organize it, compartimentalize it into smaller groupings so that others can more easily learn from it.

⚡ **POWERHOUSE**
x Brilliant

Your Brand Mix Mastery:

⚡ **POWERHOUSE** x ✶ **REBEL**

the demagogue.

You're often found leading people into battle — battle against the status quo, that is. You reject norms and instead favor ideas that help the world progress.

Work it

You are powerful because you are:

- Free-thinking
- Independent
- A lion, not a sheep
- Critical of older values and methods
- Creative

Own it

Get inspired by these kindred brands:

Jennifer Lopez - The Wing

Bring it

Amplify your strengths:

- Choose your battles and be resolute in them; you attract followers by sticking to your core beliefs (and be sure to clearly and constantly communicate what those are).

POWERHOUSE ⚡
x Rebel

Your Brand Mix Mastery:

⚡ **POWERHOUSE** x 🛡 **BFF**

the ceo.

You're the type of leader who upholds solid, tried-and-true values for your team, no matter how big or small. You're experienced, accomplished, and trusted to do a job well done.

Work it

You are powerful because you are:

- Robust
- Confident
- All about a challenge
- Good at managing people and processes
- Traditional

Own it

Get inspired by these kindred brands:

Tory Burch - Marc Benioff

Bring it

Amplify your strengths:

- If you involve your team in big decisions by being transparent at the start, you'll create buy-in and accountability that they'll be proud of in the end.

⚡ **POWERHOUSE**
x BFF

Your Brand Mix Mastery:

⚡ **POWERHOUSE** x 💎 **GEM**

the **advocate.**

People naturally follow your example, and you use your position as their frontrunner to care for and protect them. You believe that the best leaders are those who genuinely have other people's best interest in mind.

Work it

You are powerful because you are:

- Compassionate
- One to take charge in stressful situations
- Mindful of how your actions will affect other people and the environment
- Only satisfied when you've helped someone else succeed

Own it

Get inspired by these kindred brands:

Angelina Jolie - Human Rights Watch

Bring it

Amplify your strengths:

- You're not doing it for the spotlight, but you'll be more effective in empowering others if you allow them to see you in action.

POWERHOUSE ⚡
x Gem

Your Brand Mix Mastery:

⚡ **POWERHOUSE** x 🎨 **ORIGINAL**

the director.

You're normally the type to give orders, not take them, but that doesn't mean you're cold and impersonal; your artistic side allows for emotional sensitivity and careful thought.

Work it

You are powerful because you are:

- Vivid
- Natural leader
- Productive
- Creative
- One to add a fun twist to your projects

Own it

Get inspired by these kindred brands:

Shonda Rhimes - Carbon38

Bring it

Amplify your strengths:

- You can stand to be a little more creative than you typically are. Be bold in your artistic expressions; take a chance. You'll find that you'll inspire others with your courage.

⚡ **POWERHOUSE**
x Original

Your Brand Mix Mastery:

⚡ POWERHOUSE x ☼ CHARISMATIC

the charmer.

You tend to charm people with your personality and natural leadership skills. Others tend to think of you as bright, encouraging, and a pleasure to support.

Work it

You are powerful because you are:

- Magnetic
- Happy to take charge
- Humble
- Empowering
- Known for great problem-solving skills

Own it

Get inspired by these kindred brands:

Supergirl - Salesforce

Bring it

Amplify your strengths:

- Although you could boast more, you don't need to — this is one of your main attractors and why people want to follow you. Just keep doing you.

POWERHOUSE
x Charismatic ⚡

IRL INFLUENCE*HER*

Maryam Montague

Founder, M.Montague Souk, Peacock Pavilions, Agent GirlPower, Project Soar
@mmontagueliving

Photo credit: Patrick Cline

WHY WE THINK MARYAM IS A PERFECT POWERHOUSE:

First off, Maryam's "day job" is traveling to areas in the world hit by disasters as a crisis response aid worker. As if that wasn't enough, she continues to build an empire of social impact entities that provide employment, training, education, empowerment to young women, and inspiration for us all. (And p.s. she's not nearly done.) Support/be amazed: mmontague.com

What makes you excited about your work?

My company motto is *Be Good, Make Good, Do Good.* As a designer and humanitarian, I am passionate about girls' and women's rights. Accordingly, I strive to give back in everything I do, whether with my boutique hotel Peacock Pavilions, my homewares shop M.Montague Souk, my fashion brand Agent GirlPower, or my nonprofit organization Project Soar.

Can you share any struggles and how you've overcome them?

Juggling many projects, it's easy to feel overwhelmed. I manage my time using the Pomodoro technique (it's doubled my productivity!), and I meditate daily for stress. But I need more help! This year, I am hiring a graphic designer/social media manager (and in my dream world I'm also hiring an executive assistant so I can focus on the important things).

Who is your muse?

Angelina Jolie — I am inspired by her dedication to refugee advocacy, all while managing a successful career and a brood of kids. My kind of superhero.

What's next for you?

Right now I am focused on rolling out Project Soar. We are in 21 sites in Morocco and by year end we will be in 40. Additionally, we are taking Project Soar to Uganda this year. My plan is for us to be working in 10 countries within five years, serving thousands of teenage girls. Why live a small life, when you can live a big one?

Words to live by:

"I am not afraid...I was born to do this."

Joan of Arc

"**Luck has nothing to do with it.**" Serena Williams

focused

Self-Inspired

DISCIPLINED

accomplished

productive

Channel your inner:

Sheryl Sandberg

MAJOR ARCHETYPE

the boss

8

Rather than relying on external factors to motivate you, you're intrinsically driven, and you use that power to set and achieve your goals. You hold high standards for yourself and those around you, and that leads others to admire your dedication to excellence.

X MAVEN	=	Role Model
X GAMECHANGER	=	Tastemaker
X IDEALIST	=	Exceptional
X EXPLORER	=	Venturer
X POWERHOUSE	=	Champion
X BOSS	=	Paragon
X BRILLIANT	=	Highbrow
X REBEL	=	Individualist
X BFF	=	Pragmatist
X GEM	=	Upholder
X ORIGINAL	=	Mastermind
X CHARISMATIC	=	Shining Star

Your Brand Mix Mastery:

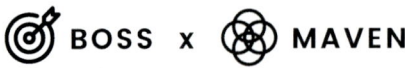 BOSS x MAVEN

the role model.

People look up to you; you're either working toward setting the standard for your field, or you've already done it. Others want to follow in your footsteps.

Work it

You are powerful because you are:

- A good example
- Accomplished
- Good at reflecting on past challenges and achievements
- Eager to educate others

Own it

Get inspired by these kindred brands:

Sheryl Sandberg - Harvard

Bring it

Amplify your strengths:

- Recognize which resources have helped you become successful, then share them with others. If you can help other people succeed, they'll be all the more confident in you.

Your Brand Mix Mastery:

 BOSS x GAMECHANGER

the tastemaker.

In a way, you help decide what people love by showing them things they've never before seen. You're always looking for ways to update something old, and everything you produce has a touch of prestige.

Work it

You are powerful because you are:

- Perceptive to people's needs
- Up-to-date on what's cool
- Go-getter
- Detail-oriented
- Forward-thinking

Own it

Get inspired by these kindred brands:

Vogue - Natalie Massenet

Bring it

Amplify your strengths:

- Subscribe to publications that predict future trends and identify/follow fellow tastemakers to stay on top of what's to come.

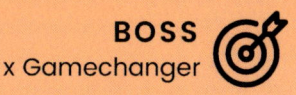

Your Brand Mix Mastery:

 **BOSS** x ♡ **IDEALIST**

the exceptional.

You're what everyone wants to be: accomplished, kind, motivated, and easy to like. You may be out there getting things done, but not without flashing a cool smile and making others feel warm and fuzzy inside.

Work it   You are powerful because you are:

- Highly productive
- Goal-oriented
- Sensitive to others' needs and wants
- Elite
- Personable

Own it   Get inspired by these kindred brands:

Misty Copeland - Hermès

Bring it   Amplify your strengths:

- Your power lies in your ability to shine without appearing ostentatious. Remain relatable by conveying a sense of awe and gratitude.

BOSS
x Idealist

Your Brand Mix Mastery:

 BOSS x EXPLORER

the venturer.

You go out of your way to discover new things, rather than settling for the old. You're accomplished without being flashy or over-the-top, but you like to keep things fresh and exciting.

Work it

You are powerful because you are:

- Curious
- Motivated
- Productive
- One to value new ideas
- Optimistic

Own it

Get inspired by these kindred brands:

Virgin Limited Edition - Jenna Lyons

Bring it

Amplify your strengths:

- People are attracted to your ability to adhere to high standards while adding a dash of fun. Be sure to insert that sense of originality and adventure now and then.

BOSS
x Explorer

Your Brand Mix Mastery:

 BOSS x POWERHOUSE

the champion.

When you're set on a goal, you stop at nothing until it's accomplished. You're known for your constant progress and your can-do attitude, which consistently pushes you toward the next win.

Work it

You are powerful because you are:

- One to set high but achievable standards
- Always impressing others
- Goal-oriented
- Highly motivated
- Confident

Own it

Get inspired by these kindred brands:

Serena Williams - Gucci

Bring it

Amplify your strengths:

- When setbacks arise, learn to go easy on yourself; look at them as opportunities to take a step back, learn and improve.

Your Brand Mix Mastery:

 BOSS x BOSS

the paragon.

Your brand is 100 percent Boss. You're the epitome of productivity, and you always look calm and cool while getting stuff done. Even the highest obstacles won't get in the way of you achieving your goals.

Work it

You are powerful because you are:

- Persistent
- Organized
- Ambitious
- Confident
- Responsible

Own it

Get inspired by these kindred brands:

Laura Vanderkam - Harry Winston

Bring it

Amplify your strengths:

- Don't let your perfectionist tendencies make you hesitate. Build momentum by breaking up larger tasks into smaller to-do lists so you feel accomplished when checking them off.

BOSS x Boss

Your Brand Mix Mastery:

 BOSS x BRILLIANT

the highbrow.

You're a sponge for information, and you like to use that data to make informed and responsible decisions that work toward your goals. As a result, people know you as someone who fearlessly accomplishes their objectives.

Work it

You are powerful because you are:

- Persistent
- Eager to learn
- Well-rounded
- Like to take action
- Responsible

Own it

Get inspired by these kindred brands:

Vanity Fair - Hillary Clinton

Bring it

Amplify your strengths:

- Being an intellectual who moves forward without looking back, you may come across as cold and impersonal. Be comfortable with showing vulnerability every now and again to be relatable.

BOSS
x Brilliant

Your Brand Mix Mastery:

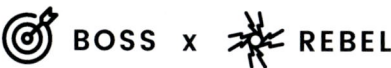 BOSS x REBEL

the individualist.

You don't waste time relying on others for help. Instead, you forge your own path, and you almost always succeed — even if you have to jump over a few hurdles.

Work it

You are powerful because you are:
- Independent
- Determined
- Accomplished
- Willing and excited to try new things
- Self-motivated

Own it

Get inspired by these kindred brands:

Gatorade - Chloe Kim

Bring it

Amplify your strengths:
- You're one who tends to work harder when someone tells you, you can't do it; you enjoy proving them wrong.

HOLLAH!

Bonus: Steps to Tribe Devotion
Find the how-to at:
orangeandbergamot.com/bonus

Your Brand Mix Mastery:

 BOSS x BFF

the pragmatist.

You're loyal, trustworthy, and a comforting force for those who seek consistency. People feel that they can rely on you to provide a useful product that they'll always be pleased with.

Work it

You are powerful because you are:
- Trustworthy
- A household name
- Reliable
- Of high integrity
- Widely loved

Own it

Get inspired by these kindred brands:

BMW - Barack Obama

Bring it

Amplify your strengths:
- Take one aspect of your work or service and deliver that to the highest caliber to stand out from the rest. Others will come to rely on your consistent quality.

BOSS
x BFF

Your Brand Mix Mastery:

 BOSS x GEM

the upholder.

You're incredibly accomplished, but you've managed to succeed by offering people things within their comfort zone. You know just what people want and need, and you give it to them in a practical way.

Work it

You are powerful because you are:

- Dependable
- No-nonsense
- Great at identifying others' needs
- Practical
- Service-oriented

Own it

Get inspired by these kindred brands:

Real Simple - The Ritz-Carlton

Bring it

Amplify your strengths:

- You're not a natural showwoman, but communicating how you continue to achieve inspires others. Feel assured knowing it's not about you, it's about them.

BOSS
x Gem

Your Brand Mix Mastery:

 BOSS x ORIGINAL

the mastermind.

You're incredibly creative; grand ideas are always swimming around in your head, and you're constantly working to turn them into something tangible. Others admire your devotion, passion, and productivity.

Work it

You are powerful because you are:

- Goal-oriented
- One to think outside the box
- Colorful
- Self-motivated
- Self-curated

Own it

Get inspired by these kindred brands:

Andy Warhol - Karl Lagerfeld

Bring it

Amplify your strengths:

- You can be your own worst critic. To keep yourself from procrastinating because of this, open yourself up to a select group of loyal allies who can help you get where you want to go.

BOSS
x Original

Your Brand Mix Mastery:

BOSS x CHARISMATIC

the shining star.

You don't have to brag for people to know you're pretty awesome — they can see it in your list of achievements. You're a friendly face, and others like you because you're humble and uplifting.

Work it

You are powerful because you are:

- Confident but not cocky
- Positive
- Hard-working
- Results-driven
- Always looking ahead

Own it

Get inspired by these kindred brands:

Marie Kondo - Yusra Mardini

Bring it

Amplify your strengths:

- Part of your attraction is your ability to look at falls as opportunities to shine. Your fans can rely on you to always share the bright side and what you learned from it, looking ahead.

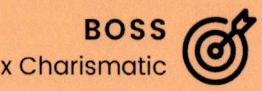

BOSS
x Charismatic

IRL INFLUENCE*HER*

Kat Tanita

Founder, With Love From Kat
@kattanita

Photo credits: Carly Tumen (above)
Jessica Alexander (right)

WHY WE THINK KAT IS A PERFECT BOSS:

This girl's got goals...and can't stop, won't stop creating and producing so that she can share her finds with her audience. Like a true "boss" brand, Kat holds the highest standards for herself, evident in everything she touches. No surprise that fellow boss brands like Burberry and Audi would collaborate with her, and *Elle* and *Harper's Bazaar* would feature her. What a boss. withlovefromkat.com

What makes you excited about your work?
Since I was little, I've always been an extremely creative person, so being able to be creative every single day as an adult is a dream! I also love being able to connect with like minded women all over the world.

Can you share any struggles and how you've overcome them?
It's been both exciting and scary creating my own career path. The blogging industry is relatively new so there was never any manual or guidebook or class I could take, I just had to learn as I went and dive in head first. I have taken many risks in my career and many of them have luckily paid off! I think my strong work ethic, intuition and authenticity has helped me stay relevant and create a lasting career.

Who is your muse?
My grandmother. She sewed all of her own clothes and was an extremely hands on, creative person. She had a gracefulness and elegance about her - and was always so humble. She was the most compassionate person I know and volunteered or helped others on a daily basis.

What's next for you?
I just wrote a cookbook! I healed my digestion problems through food and realized that food was the key to glowing skin, a healthy body, a happy mind. I am so excited to share my journey and my solutions with other women who want to look and feel their best without compromising taste. This book will combine recipes with decor tips, and my favorite self care practices as well! This is only the beginning of the wellness empire I am working on building and I am thrilled to be expanding my site to include more wellness tips and really connect with my audience in a deeper, more meaningful way.

Words to live by:

"Go confidently in the direction of your dreams. Live the life you've imagined." Henry David Thoreau

> "What people say isn't going to stop me. I have to do things for myself." Kate Moss

brave

SELF-ASSURED

forging your own destiny

changemaking

Inspirational

Channel your inner:

Malala Yousafzai

MAJOR ARCHETYPE

the rebel

9

You march to the beat of your own drum. You'd rather stand out than blend in, and it shows in the things you do and create. You're confident enough in your own abilities that you don't worry about what others think — you just do what you know is right.

X MAVEN	=	Icon
X GAMECHANGER	=	Revolutionary
X IDEALIST	=	Lone Wolf
X EXPLORER	=	Experimenter
X POWERHOUSE	=	Antihero
X BOSS	=	Entrepreneur
X BRILLIANT	=	Daredevil
X REBEL	=	Nonconformist
X BFF	=	Resilient
X GEM	=	Rebel with a Cause
X ORIGINAL	=	Eccentric
X CHARISMATIC	=	Satirist

Your Brand Mix Mastery:

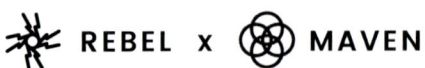 REBEL x MAVEN

the icon.

You are the ultimate "walk the walk, not just talk the talk." You inspire others by being willing to be bold and take risks. Your actions are just as loud as your words.

Work it

You are powerful because you are:
- Brave
- Spirited
- Passionate
- Determined
- Stick with what you believe in

Own it

Get inspired by these kindred brands:

Malala Yousafzai - Noam Chomsky

Bring it

Amplify your strengths:
- Use unconventional methods of passing on information, as this makes you all the more striking.

REBEL
x Maven

Your Brand Mix Mastery:

 REBEL x GAMECHANGER

the revolutionary.

You like to stray from the beaten path and go for something new; the "same old stuff" doesn't interest you. You're always looking for ways to improve things that already exist or create something original.

Work it

You are powerful because you are:

- Courageous
- Independent
- Creative
- Never settle for mediocrity
- Broad-minded

Own it

Get inspired by these kindred brands:

Amy Schumer - CrossFit

Bring it

Amplify your strengths:

- Part of your appeal is in rallying against what isn't working. But you also need to communicate how you would change it (and then do it, to prove you're right…metrics are key).

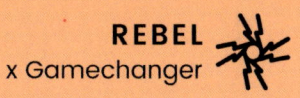

REBEL
x Gamechanger

Your Brand Mix Mastery:

 REBEL x IDEALIST

the lone wolf.

You're the definition of mysterious, but that makes you all the more appealing. You're highly independent and you forge your own path; this confidence keeps people coming back.

Work it

You are powerful because you are:

- One to leave things to the imagination
- Individualist
- A believer that rules were made to be broken
- Wistful
- Never hesitate to chase your dreams

Own it

Get inspired by these kindred brands:

Kate Moss - Soho House

Bring it

Amplify your strengths:

- People are attracted to you because you are selective with what you choose to reveal. Stand out from the pack by cultivating curiosity.

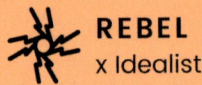

REBEL
x Idealist

HOLLAH!

Bonus: Productivity Hacks
Find our top tips at:
orangeandbergamot.com/bonus

Your Brand Mix Mastery:

 REBEL x EXPLORER

the experimenter.

You're always saying "Why not?" — after all, trial and error is far better than never having tried at all. You inspire others with your courage and adaptive nature.

Work it

You are powerful because you are:

- A challenge-lover
- Inquisitive
- Eager to learn
- Risk-taking
- Hopeful

Own it

Get inspired by these kindred brands:

Tiffany Haddish - Slack

Bring it

Amplify your strengths:

- Identify pain points in your industry and brainstorm ways to try something different, even if you don't have it all figured out yet. "Iteration" is your friend.

REBEL x Explorer

Your Brand Mix Mastery:

 REBEL x POWERHOUSE

the antihero.

No one quite expected you to come as far as you have — after all, you don't fit the typical definition of the hero — but nonetheless, you've managed to make yourself into something people know about and love. Your qualities are unique, making them particularly powerful.

Work it

You are powerful because you are:

- Unconventional
- Strong-willed
- Mysterious
- A quiet planner
- Provocative

Own it

Get inspired by these kindred brands:

Madonna - *Game of Thrones*

Bring it

Amplify your strengths:

- You have been able to attract others by your constant ability to surprise them all. Do the unexpected every once in a while to throw them off and keep them enticed.

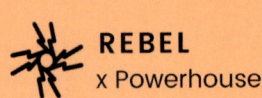

Your Brand Mix Mastery:

 REBEL x BOSS

the entrepreneur.

You hate to follow in others' footsteps; instead, you blaze your own trail and create things that other people have never even thought of before. You prefer to lead the way, not wait for someone else to.

Work it

You are powerful because you are:

- Ambitious
- Revolutionary
- Nonconforming
- Free-thinking
- Productive

Own it

Get inspired by these kindred brands:

Toni Ko - Gary Vaynerchuk

Bring it

Amplify your strengths:

- You never stop asking questions. What sets you apart is you create your own answers. Be transparent with your audience about the dialogue that led you to them; you'll build loyalty.

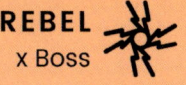

Your Brand Mix Mastery:

 REBEL x BRILLIANT

the daredevil.

You do things others may consider risky or daring, but they're always carefully calculated based on information you've gathered. You enjoy how exhilarating each win is when you've had to jump numerous hurdles to get there.

Work it

You are powerful because you are:

- Studious
- A planner, not random
- Eager to try new things
- Always trying to be the "first" at something
- Ambitious

Own it

Get inspired by these kindred brands:

Larry Ellison - PayPal

Bring it

Amplify your strengths:

- Be knowledgeable of changing conditions by inserting processes of gathering metrics along the way. This will help you remain resilient, adaptable, and able to take more risks.

REBEL
x Brilliant

Your Brand Mix Mastery:

 REBEL x REBEL

the nonconformist.

Your brand is 100 percent Rebel at heart. You pride yourself on your history of forging your own path and your ability to make things happen your way. You believe that rules were made to be broken.

Work it

You are powerful because you are:

- Motivated
- Individualist
- Persevering
- Aware
- Revolutionary

Own it

Get inspired by these kindred brands:

Harley Davidson - Cara Delevingne

Bring it

Amplify your strengths:

- You attract your tribe by constantly challenging the status quo. But maintain focus in your rebellions; this will help you gain a following and enlarge your platform for the change you seek.

Your Brand Mix Mastery:

 REBEL x BFF

the resilient.

You've fought hard to be where you stand now, and others admire you for it. You may not have taken the road most traveled, but you (and those who support you) believe you're much cooler and stronger for taking a unique path.

Work it

You are powerful because you are:

- Self-reliant
- Confident
- Unafraid to stand out
- Due to be a household name (if not already)
- Inspiring

Own it

Get inspired by these kindred brands:

Women's March - *Harper's Bazaar*

Bring it

Amplify your strengths:

- Others continue to be drawn to you because you've always shown a certain spunk and willingness to take risks. It's ok to point to these out in order for them to see the road you did travel.

Your Brand Mix Mastery:

 REBEL x GEM

the rebel with a cause.

You're compassionate and frequently choose to protect others using new or unconventional methods. You would rather do what you feel is right than stick to the status quo.

Work it

You are powerful because you are:

- Brave
- Fight for what you believe in
- Committed to helping others
- Would rather be a "lion" than a "sheep"
- Fiercely independent

Own it

Get inspired by these kindred brands:

MeToo - Emma Gonzalez

Bring it

Amplify your strengths:

- You know why you do what you. Make sure you communicate that with a clear message so that others see not only the passion behind it, but the reasons behind it. (Stats are a plus!)

REBEL x Gem

Your Brand Mix Mastery:

 REBEL x ORIGINAL

the eccentric.

You're quirky and fun, and to many, you're a breath of fresh air. You create unconventional things using unconventional methods, and you're proud of it.

Work it

You are powerful because you are:

- Unique
- Outgoing
- Creative
- Thoughtful
- Bright

Own it

Get inspired by these kindred brands:

Cirque du Soleil - Vivienne Westwood

Bring it

Amplify your strengths:

- Part of being eccentric is knowing what else is out there, in order to be different and get inspired. Get yourself to the latest art shows, contemporary museums, live performances, etc. to fuel your creative juices.

REBEL
x Original

Your Brand Mix Mastery:

 REBEL x CHARISMATIC

the satirist.

You like to push your sense of humor to the farthest reaches, but the end product is something fresh — something others eat right up. You pride yourself on your wit.

Work it

You are powerful because you are:

- Unafraid to tell the truth
- Funny
- Realistic in your worldview
- Original
- Entertaining

Own it

Get inspired by these kindred brands:

Chelsea Handler - *The Daily Show*

Bring it

Amplify your strengths:

- Your style isn't for everyone and that's ok. Don't dilute your pull by trying to be everything to everyone. Stay true to your core and you'll attract the right tribe.

IRL INFLUENCE*HER*

Jeni Castro

Founder, Bronzed Bunny @bronzedbunny
Co-Founder, Coffee Dose @coffeedosecm

Photo credit: Studio 1208

WHY WE THINK JENI IS A PERFECT REBEL:

Jeni has looked at two industries (so far!) — waxing salons and coffee houses — and has identified how to stand out by creating completely different experiences from the norm. She continues to challenge the status quo not by just talking about it, but by getting out there and doing it.

What makes you excited about your work?
I have created an experience unlike any other in the tanning and waxing space. We greet our clients with pink champagne and cater to them as if they are the only ones in the building. You get to choose your own chick flick in the sugar rooms. It's like hanging out with your girlfriends rather than that scary sterile white room that a lot of other spas offer. From the minute you walk in you're having fun. Not a lot of people get to say that about their business.

Can you share any struggles and how you've overcome them?
Staff. There was a period of time when I gave too much of myself to people. I trusted that their hearts were in the right place. Being that trusting person allowed me to put my business and my livelihood in jeopardy. I will never do that again.

Who is your muse?
Alli Webb. She has created the ultimate hang out spot! Every aspect of what she has built has her personal touch, that is so important. Her products, her style of training, everything is 100% consistent. I've gone thru so much franchising my concept. I've learned a lot and I'm still learning everyday. Drybar keeps my head in the game. It's something I strive for.

What's next for you?
The coffee business. We opened our first cafe, Coffee Dose, in Costa Mesa about 3 months ago and I'm OBSESSED! I love being able to create and grow a new brand!

Words to live by:

"Thoughts become things." Mike Dooley

I've created the majority of what I have, not just the material things, but every good thing I have in my life, I manifested. I thought about what I wanted every single day. I imagined how I would feel having those things, enjoying those things...all the way down to the love of my life. We dated when I was 19 and reunited after 14 years. We're married now with a toddler and a baby on the way. I've never been more complete in my whole life.

> "Oh, it's not really gambling when you never lose." — Jennifer Aniston

Timeless

trustworthy

consistent

dependable

SUPPORTIVE

Channel your inner:

Reese Witherspoon

MAJOR ARCHETYPE

10

the BFF

You're reassuring, comforting, and loved by nearly everyone because you work to earn others' trust. People come to you because they know they can always rely on you. You don't believe in extravagance or frivolities; instead, you'd rather give people what you know they want and need.

X MAVEN	=	Principal
X GAMECHANGER	=	Innovator
X IDEALIST	=	Anchor
X EXPLORER	=	Researcher
X POWERHOUSE	=	Sheriff
X BOSS	=	Dependable
X BRILLIANT	=	Level Head
X REBEL	=	Underdog
X BFF	=	Traditionalist
X GEM	=	Mainstay
X ORIGINAL	=	Artisan
X CHARISMATIC	=	Popular

Your Brand Mix Mastery:

 BFF x MAVEN

the principal.

You love sharing information and experiences with others in tried-and-true ways. People trust your judgment and often seek your wisdom when they're feeling stuck.

Work it

You are powerful because you are:

- Consider all sides of an issue or debate
- Level-headed
- Educated
- Clever
- "Better to be safe than sorry" mindset

Own it

Get inspired by these kindred brands:

How I Built This - Joyce Chang

Bring it

Optimize your strengths:

- You would never offer advice there wasn't a track record behind it. Highlight this fact by incorporating supporting evidence or stories, especially your own.

BFF x Maven

Your Brand Mix Mastery:

the innovator.

You're an innovator in the traditional sense of the word — you take ideas and data and turn them into fascinating realities. People admire your creativity and willingness to think outside the box.

Work it

You are powerful because you are:
- Unafraid to experiment
- Love to try new things
- Open-minded
- Reliable
- Trustworthy

Own it

Get inspired by these kindred brands:

Stitch Fix - Amazon Prime

Bring it

Optimize your strengths:
- You thrive off of new ideas, but to build trust, it's crucial to be transparent with your process so that others can see what they can expect.

BFF x Gamechanger

Your Brand Mix Mastery:

 BFF x IDEALIST

the anchor.

You are a comforting, familiar, smiling face that puts others at ease. People can rely on you for positive support and security. You're very easy to trust.

Work it

You are powerful because you are:

- Warm
- One to carry an aura of stability
- Understanding
- Compassionate
- Humble

Own it

Get inspired by these kindred brands:

Leslie Mann - Starbucks

Bring it

Optimize your strengths:

- Your power lies in the fact that you are consistently a delightful experience. Be sure to uphold your standards of quality to remain so.

BFF x Idealist

HOLLAH!

Bonus: What do they really want?
Get the insider info at:
orangeandbergamot.com/bonus

Your Brand Mix Mastery:

 BFF x EXPLORER

the researcher.

You're eager to learn new things and share them with your peers. You carry a cheerful yet humble attitude that easily draws people in.

Work it   You are powerful because you are:

- Adventurous
- Experience-driven
- Open-minded
- Authentic
- Resourceful

Own it   Get inspired by these kindred brands:

Giada de Laurentiis - Subaru

Bring it   Optimize your strengths:

- Part of your appeal is in your openness to discovery, but people are attracted to you because they feel safe knowing you've done your homework. Show that you have.

BFF x Explorer

Your Brand Mix Mastery:

BFF x POWERHOUSE

the sheriff.

You follow rules to a "T" — you're most productive that way. When it comes to leading others, you're a bit of a classicist; certain methods are tried-and-true, so it's best that you stick with them.

Work it

You are powerful because you are:

- Knowledgable of what works and what doesn't
- Trustworthy
- Timeless
- One to prefer quality over quantity
- Able to easily get on people's "good side"

Own it

Get inspired by these kindred brands:

Nordstrom - Coca-Cola

Bring it

Optimize your strengths:

- Over time you've already proven you are worthy of others' trust. Now's the time to turn the focus on quality. Document your processes, and be willing to learn and be adaptable when an issue arises. You're always in control of a situation.

BFF x Powerhouse

Your Brand Mix Mastery:

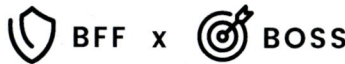 BFF x BOSS

the dependable.

You're who people go to when they need inspiration or a kickstart for something new and daunting. Others admire your ability to get stuff done with little to no hesitation, with quality and care.

Work it

You are powerful because you are:

- Quality-driven
- Self-assured
- Organized
- Honest
- Reliable

Own it

Get inspired by these kindred brands:

J.Crew   -   Jessica Alba

Bring it

Optimize your strengths:

- Stay in touch with your core audience's changing needs to always improve. You can do this via surveys, social media engagement, and speaking directly with your customers or clients.

Your Brand Mix Mastery:

 BFF x BRILLIANT

the level head.

In times of chaos, you're a stable and comforting force for good. People are drawn to your ability to look at issues from all sides and with a sensible mindset.

Work it

You are powerful because you are:

- Considerate
- Smart
- Emotionally intelligent
- Dependable
- Practical

Own it

Get inspired by these kindred brands:

NYT Best Sellers List - Microsoft

Bring it

Optimize your strengths:

- Ask yourself if all the features of your product or service are truly necessary. Make sure to only offer what people need — customers and clients like you because you avoid fluff.

Your Brand Mix Mastery:

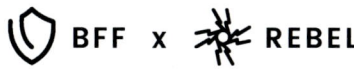

the underdog.

You don't need the spotlight to be on you, but you never fail to come through when you're needed. Others may have doubted you in the past, but you always prove them wrong with your will to do what you feel is right.

Work it

You are powerful because you are:
- Faithful
- Strong
- Dependable
- Intelligent
- Adventurous

Own it

Get inspired by these kindred brands:

MAKERS - Alicia Keys

Bring it

Optimize your strengths:
- You've come to expect some pushback, so be ready to highlight your hard work and achievements to the table. You'll continue to earn trust amongst your peers.

BFF
x Rebel

Your Brand Mix Mastery:

🛡 BFF x 🛡 BFF

the traditionalist.

Your brand is 100 percent BFF at heart. You value traditional methods and ideals and understand that your audience does as well. You stay "within your lane" and give people what they're comfortable with, which makes you immensely reliable.

Work it

You are powerful because you are:

- Comforting
- Established
- Straight-shooting
- Content
- Dependable

Own it

Get inspired by these kindred brands:

Le Creuset - UPS

Bring it

Optimize your strengths:

- Customer service is key. Be sure your policies or values are clearly stated and be willing to go above and beyond to ensure someone's satisfaction. Money Back Guarantees go a long way.

Your Brand Mix Mastery:

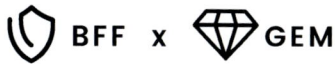 BFF x GEM

the mainstay.

Like a comfort food, people are immediately put at ease by your presence. They know they can go to you when they're in a difficult situation. At best, you'll have resources to give them; at the least, you'll offer kind and comforting words of advice.

Work it

You are powerful because you are:
- Kind-hearted
- Supportive
- Honest
- Thoughtful
- Reliable

Own it

Get inspired by these kindred brands:

Reese Witherspoon - Campbell Soup Company

Bring it

Optimize your strengths:
- Response time is critical in building trust. Even if you don't have all the answers for someone right away, let them know you'll get back to them (and do).

Your Brand Mix Mastery:

 BFF x ORIGINAL

the artisan.

You offer services or products that are easily loved by all. Everything you produce has sweet details and little features that "wow" your customers.

Work it

You are powerful because you are:
- Consistent
- Creative
- High-quality
- Appeal to people's emotions
- Colorful

Own it

Get inspired by these kindred brands:

Anthropologie - Gray Malin

Bring it

Optimize your strengths:
- Keep it consistently fresh; brainstorm ways in which you can add an extra dose of delight for people, whether that's through personal touches or little thoughtful surprises.

BFF x Original

Your Brand Mix Mastery:

BFF x CHARISMATIC

the popular.

You have a humble and content outlook on life that keeps you level-headed, but also gets you through the toughest of times. You handle obstacles swiftly; they're water off a duck's back.

Work it
You are powerful because you are:
- Dependable
- Confident
- Accomplished
- Kind
- Organized

Own it
Get inspired by these kindred brands:

Jennifer Aniston - Southwest Airlines

Bring it
Optimize your strengths:
- You don't take yourself too seriously and that is inspiring for others. Your resilience and "all will be ok" attitude ease tense situations. Be the light at the end of the tunnel.

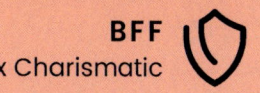
BFF x Charismatic

IRL INFLUENCE*HER*

Danielle Moss

Co-Founder,
The Everygirl Media Group
@theeverygirl_ @theeverymom
@daniellemoss_

Photo credits:
Katie Kett Photography (left)
Stoffer Photography (above)

WHY WE THINK DANIELLE IS A PERFECT BFF:
Danielle, with co-founder Alaina Kaczmarski, created a platform for fellow young women; *The Everygirl* was quickly listed on Forbes' "Top 10 Websites for Millennial Women." She consistently strives to create thoughtful, quality content that any girl can relate to and rely on, and is energized by its impact. We know to expect no less than the best. danielle-moss.com, theeverygirl.com, theeverymom.com

What makes you excited about your work?
When readers email to share how *The Everygirl* or my personal blog have inspired them, I know I'm doing exactly what I was meant to do.

Can you share any struggles and how you've overcome them?
I spent my 20's feeling so lost both professionally and personally. It took growing up, creating a job I love, and lots of "me" time before I finally had a better sense of who I was and what I wanted. I've also struggled with anxiety and put so much pressure on myself for everything to be perfect. I think getting older taught me to reevaluate things, and I finally learned to slow down and relax.

Who is your muse?
I've been lucky to surround myself with creative friends who all inspire me to do my best work.

What's next for you?
I just had my first baby and launched *The Everymom*, and it's been exciting to watch our company grow. So I'll be entering this new chapter: learning to navigate running two websites, a personal blog, and motherhood. I've felt very pulled to use my blog and social media to help other young women feel inspired and less alone, so I'm excited to do more of that, and to continue to grow The Everygirl Media Group.

Words to live by:

"I've learned that people will forget what you said, people will forget what you did, but people will never forget how you made them feel." Maya Angelou

"**Don't ever let a soul in the world tell you that you can't be exactly who you are.**" Lady Gaga

comforting

protective

EMPATHETIC

giving

Nurturing

Channel your inner:
Megan Markle

MAJOR ARCHETYPE

11

the gem

You often put others' needs before your own and consider the "greater good" with everything you do. People come to you for love and comfort, and you're happy to provide that support. Few are as good at reading others' needs as you are, and it gives you great joy if you can meet them. You're often seen as selfless, and you're actually much more comfortable giving than receiving.

X MAVEN	=	Counselor
X GAMECHANGER	=	Ally
X IDEALIST	=	Companion
X EXPLORER	=	Cultivator
X POWERHOUSE	=	Altruist
X BOSS	=	Benefactor
X BRILLIANT	=	Trainer
X REBEL	=	Tough Lover
X BFF	=	Good Samaritan
X GEM	=	Humanitarian
X ORIGINAL	=	Hippie
X CHARISMATIC	=	Glow

Your Brand Mix Mastery:

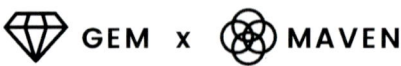 GEM x MAVEN

the counselor.

You're the type people go to for guidance, and also the type people strive to be. Your main drive is a need to help, protect, and educate others so that they can succeed.

Work it

You are powerful because you are:

- Good at providing support at the right time
- Patient
- Empowering
- Protective
- Wise

Own it

Get inspired by these kindred brands:

UNICEF - Christy Turlington

Bring it

Amplify your strengths:

- You're good at what you do and want to teach others to be the same. Document and share your processes — even if it seems mundane to you — to take people step-by-step. It's less overwhelming and will help give them a feeling of accomplishment.

GEM
x Maven

Your Brand Mix Mastery:

the ally.

You want the future to be a better place and time, and as a result, you use innovation to effect the necessary change. You're always looking ahead for ways to help people, whether it's now or in the time to come.

Work it

You are powerful because you are:

- Forward-thinking
- Passionate
- Attentive
- Socially aware
- Contemporary

Own it

Get inspired by these kindred brands:

Jasmine Crowe (Goodr Co.) - Enrou

Bring it

Amplify your strengths:

- Reach out to your network, spread your passion for your mission and get a little wacky with your solutions; you attract others by being bold (not safe), in the service of others.

Your Brand Mix Mastery:

 **GEM** x **IDEALIST**

the companion.

Your passion is passion, as well as taking care of others. You emit love and light wherever you go. People feel safe and cared for in your presence.

Work it

You are powerful because you are:

- A gentle soul
- Emotionally-driven
- Often put others' needs before your own
- Considerate
- Kind

Own it

Get inspired by these kindred brands:

charity: water - Adele

Bring it

Amplify your strengths:

- Others know they can rely on your warmth and compassion to always lift them up. You can be even more effective if you're proactive rather than just reactive: think ahead to what others might need.

GEM
x Idealist

Your Brand Mix Mastery:

 **GEM x EXPLORER**

the cultivator.

You are always seeking the truth, and feel a great sense of responsibility to continuously do the right thing. You care a great deal about others, and you will always make sure everyone is on the same page.

Work it

You are powerful because you are:

- Noble
- Known for a strong work ethic
- Caring
- Trustworthy
- A Fast learner

Own it

Get inspired by these kindred brands:

Global Citizen - Lady Gaga

Bring it

Amplify your strengths:

- Engage and activate your core audience with tangible action steps they can take to be part of a larger initiative.

Your Brand Mix Mastery:

◆ GEM x ⚡ POWERHOUSE

the altruist.

You are a caregiver by nature, but you stand your ground when necessary. You are incredibly generous and want what is best for both you and others. You won't back down when it means others will be impacted negatively.

Work it

You are powerful because you are:

- Selfless
- Emotionally tough
- Stable
- Dependable
- A great listener

Own it

Get inspired by these kindred brands:

Megan Markle - Girl Effect

Bring it

Amplify your strengths:

- You are powerful in your ability to embolden others to join your cause….but not with infographics and statistics. Rather, use personal stories and real-life inspirations for the biggest impact.

Your Brand Mix Mastery:

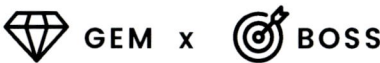 GEM x BOSS

the benefactor.

You go above and beyond in all that you do. You do it not only for yourself, but the ones that you love. You're capable of assisting others without aiming the spotlight at yourself.

Work it

You are powerful because you are:

- Selfless
- Highly accomplished
- Affluent
- Analytical
- Empathetic

Own it

Get inspired by these kindred brands:

The Association of Junior Leagues International - Jackie O.

Bring it

Amplify your strengths:

- You are particulary skilled at rallying the troops with your transparency and selfless determination. Agendas, strategic plans, and metrics go a long way to build teamwork.

HOLLAH!

Bonus: Reading List
Find our top reco's for biz books at:
orangeandbergamot.com/bonus

Your Brand Mix Mastery:

GEM x BRILLIANT

the trainer.

Your #1 is others before yourself, and you use your skills in strategic evaluation and planning to help in that effort. Others are drawn to your natural ability to use information for good.

Work it

You are powerful because you are:
- Helpful
- Optimistic
- Compassionate
- A critical thinker
- Determined

Own it

Get inspired by these kindred brands:

Naya Health - Indra Nooyi

Bring it

Amplify your strengths:
- People who are naturally selfless aren't always the best planners because they often react to situations around them. You are most effective when you can use your intellect to plan ahead for others.

GEM x Brilliant

Your Brand Mix Mastery:

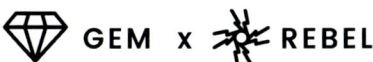 GEM x REBEL

the tough lover.

You have a big heart, but you know that life is the greatest teacher of all — and sometimes you have to let the ones you love learn that too, on their own. You value experience and are full of wisdom.

Work it

You are powerful because you are:

- Smart
- Loving
- Proud of your own achievements and others'
- Strong
- Reliable

Own it

Get inspired by these kindred brands:

Gloria Steinem - Time's Up

Bring it

Amplify your strengths:

- You are not afraid to tackle issues head on, but don't forget that others don't always have your courage and strength. Provide opportunites for small commitments and "ease of entry" to bring them in.

GEM x Rebel

Your Brand Mix Mastery:

 GEM x BFF

the good samaritan.

You aren't trying to look like a hero, but when someone needs you, you drop everything to help. People know they can consistently count on you for care and compassion, and you're humbly happy to be of service.

Work it

You are powerful because you are:

- Caring
- Modest
- Often put others' needs ahead of your own
- Advocate for the less visible or less fortunate
- Discreet and unassuming

Own it

Get inspired by these kindred brands:

The Red Cross - Princess Diana

Bring it

Amplify your strengths:

- You naturally don't feel comfortable tooting your own horn, but it's important to provide transparency in your efforts to establish trust with your audience. Let them see what you do behind the scenes.

Your Brand Mix Mastery:

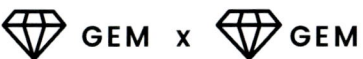 GEM x GEM

the humanitarian.

Your brand is 100 percent Gem at heart. You know that your purpose is to help and care for others, and your ability to do so is renowned. You give people hope with your commitment to making the world a better place.

Work it

You are powerful because you are:

- Reliable
- Understanding
- Use your privilege to help others
- Humble
- Kind

Own it

Get inspired by these kindred brands:

U.N. Refugee Agency - Mother Teresa

Bring it

Amplify your strengths:

- You're the ultimate mother hen, which also means you have a tendency to forget to take care of yourself. Think of it this way: if you don't, you'll have others worrying about you. And you'd rather the focus be on them, not you.

Your Brand Mix Mastery:

 **GEM** x **ORIGINAL**

the hippie.

You love to spread love, especially if it's through something you've created yourself. Your ideal world is one in which people get along and support one another through thick and thin.

Work it

You are powerful because you are:

- Hopeful
- Kind
- Creative
- Considerate of others' goals and feelings
- Fun-loving

Own it

Get inspired by these kindred brands:

Coachella - Vanessa Hudgens

Bring it

Amplify your strengths:

- You attract others by following your own rules, and they tend to be ones that are eco conscious and socially aware. Highlight them; a purpose behind what you do carries clout and depth.

Your Brand Mix Mastery:

the glow.

You're all about making people smile, and you accomplish this best with your authenticity and generosity. You have a light about you that shines on people when they need it most.

Work it

You are powerful because you are:

- One to put others before yourself
- Optimistic
- Family-friendly
- Comforting
- Supportive

Own it

Get inspired by these kindred brands:

Chobani - Julia Roberts

Bring it

Amplify your strengths:

- Use your positivity and good sense of humor to lift others up when they're down. Show you care, whether that's directly to individuals or through being vocal about and visible in social impact initiatives.

GEM
x Charismatic

IRL INFLUENCE*HER*

Amy Eldon Turteltaub

Activist & Co-Founder,
Creative Visions
@cvfoundation

Photo credit: Jennifer Daigle

WHY WE THINK AMY IS A PERFECT GEM:

Although it runs in her blood, a life in service of a greater good became Amy's purpose after a family tragedy. As an Emmy and Oscar-nominated filmmaker, she is tireless in her efforts to support and share global stories of ordinary people changing their worlds, empowering others to do the same. Gracious, selfless and diligent for the cause, Amy is a true gem. creativevisions.org

What makes you excited about your work?
I love supporting our program, *Rock Your World*, which empowers the next generation of creative activists...young people who will ultimately turn things around.

Can you share any struggles and how you've overcome them?
When I was 19 my brother Dan was killed while on assignment as a photojournalist in Somalia. After going through the pain of his death, I realized I could survive just about anything. My worst nightmare had become a reality, but I was okay.

Death has a way of pulling into sharper focus what really matters in life, although of course as time goes on we again get caught up in silly insignificant things. Now when confronted with major challenges, I try to remember the saying, "this too shall pass," and then I call upon my circle of wise women to determine if my inner voice is accurate or totally insane.

Who is your muse?
My grandmother, Louise Knapp, who lived a life dedicated to service to her family, her community and the world. Despite living in Iowa, she was a "global soul," traveling to 77 countries and sponsoring many international students. My grandmother had a wicked sense of humor — and she loved us all "just the way we are." I try to channel her patience when I want to strangle one of my kids.

What's next for you?
I have absolutely no idea. As my brother would say, "the journey is the destination."

Words to live by:

"Bless and release."

> "Get at least eight hours of beauty sleep. Nine if you're ugly." Betty White

Clever

WITTY

funny

light-hearted

resilient

Channel your inner: *Tina Fey*

MAJOR ARCHETYPE 12

the charismatic

You're incredibly personable, with a bright outlook and a great sense of humor. People can rely on you to find a silver lining in any situation or make them laugh, even after the toughest days. You love winning people over with your wit and charm, and know you've done so when you see that smile.

X MAVEN	=	Friend
X GAMECHANGER	=	Modernist
X IDEALIST	=	Light-Hearted
X EXPLORER	=	Open Heart
X POWERHOUSE	=	Genuine
X BOSS	=	Endurer
X BRILLIANT	=	Wit
X REBEL	=	Anarchist
X BFF	=	Congenial
X GEM	=	Crystal
X ORIGINAL	=	Humorist
X CHARISMATIC	=	Comic

Your Brand Mix Mastery:

the friend.

You provide an uplifting spirit and a guiding hand, often desiring to mentor your peers and give them advice even in the darkest of times. You always have a kind word to say and are willing to give others a gentle push in the right direction.

Work it

You are powerful because you are:

- Engaging
- Sensible
- Encouraging
- Able to put a positive spin on almost anything
- Personable

Own it

Get inspired by these kindred brands:

The Skimm - Elizabeth Banks

Bring it

Amplify your strengths:

- You have an innate ability to see what others may miss, often the good in situations. Break it down in bite-sized nuggets and as always, add a light-hearted touch.

CHARISMATIC
x Maven

Your Brand Mix Mastery:

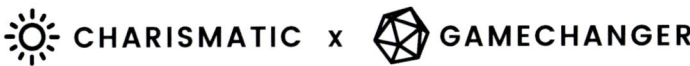

CHARISMATIC x GAMECHANGER

the modernist.

Your ideas are bright, optimistic, and progressive. Others admire your ability to get creative with what you put out. You especially enjoy innovating solutions that make things easier for everyone.

Work it

You are powerful because you are:

- Forward-thinking
- Always looking for ways to improve older ideas
- Positive
- Cheerful
- Entertaining

Own it

Get inspired by these kindred brands:

Postmates - IKEA

Bring it

Amplify your strengths:

- You are one to always see the positives in new ideas, but be sure to get outside opinions from questioners (like Rebels) or fact-checkers (like Brilliants) to test out your ideas. You may miss unintended consequences.

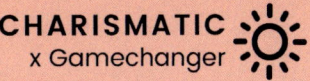

Your Brand Mix Mastery:

the light-hearted.

You're a glass-mostly-full person, and a little rain on your parade won't stop you from accomplishing your goals. You know that positivity isn't everybody's cup of tea, but you're happy to share the love with anyone who's willing to listen.

Work it

You are powerful because you are:

- Bubbly
- Easygoing
- Always looking for the "bright side"
- Joyful
- Energetic

Own it

Get inspired by these kindred brands:

Kate Hudson - Dollar Shave Club

Bring it

Amplify your strengths:

- Your confidence that "everything's gonna be alright" inspires others to plow through. Lead with positivity, and they'll follow.

CHARISMATIC
x Idealist

Your Brand Mix Mastery:

CHARISMATIC x EXPLORER

the open heart.

Your arms are as open as your heart. You recognize the importance of being available to everybody around you so that you can offer a supportive shoulder whenever they need it.

Work it

You are powerful because you are:

- Unafraid of showing compassion
- One to enjoy reaching out to people
- Ready to love
- Listener
- Kind

Own it

Get inspired by these kindred brands:

Bumble - Gal Gadot

Bring it

Amplify your strengths:

- You attract others with your belief in the best in people. Encourage them to be their best selves by providing opportunities for them to highlight their positives, always.

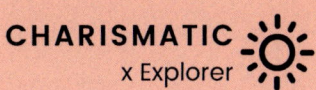

Your Brand Mix Mastery:

☀ CHARISMATIC x ⚡ POWERHOUSE

the genuine.

You wear your heart on your sleeve, and you keep no secrets from anybody. You are unabashed in telling others, "What you see is what you get." You always say that honesty is the best policy, and it's served you well.

Work it

You are powerful because you are:

- Honest
- Encourage sincerity
- Forthright
- Make friends easily
- Inspire people to "live out loud"

Own it

Get inspired by these kindred brands:

Chrissy Teigen - Spanx

Bring it

Amplify your strengths:

- You have a knack for taking something complicated or uncomfortable and by baring it all, you disarm and connect with your audience. They love your raw honesty.

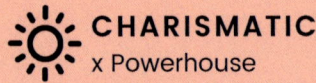

Your Brand Mix Mastery:

the endurer.

Your overall good humor attracts valuable human connections and success. Obstacles rarely block you from achieving your goals; instead, you find silver linings and let your troubles roll right off your back.

Work it

You are powerful because you are:

- Optimistic
- Persevere even when you face major hurdles
- Great sense of humor
- A confident attitude that attracts others
- Commited to success

Own it

Get inspired by these kindred brands:

Mirai Nagasu - Mindy Kaling

Bring it

Amplify your strengths:

- Your motto: "If you stumble, make it part of the dance." You know what you want and how to get there, but how you share your falls along the way remind others that they can get to the finish line too.

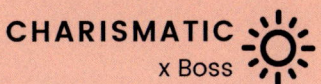

Your Brand Mix Mastery:

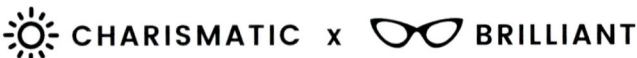 CHARISMATIC x BRILLIANT

the wit.

You are quick to the draw with new ideas and a sense of what works in every situation. On the rare occasion your first thought doesn't work out, you can break it down and insert just the right amount of "fix" to solve it for the next time.

Work it

You are powerful because you are:

- Quick thinker
- Draw attention to yourself
- Witty
- Prudent
- Considerate

Own it

Get inspired by these kindred brands:

Tina Fey - *Arrested Development*

Bring it

Amplify your strengths:

- How you stay one witty step ahead is by having your finger on the pulse of pop culture and current affairs. Read dailies, periodicals, gossip mags, and yes, what's trending on Twitter.

Your Brand Mix Mastery:

 CHARISMATIC x REBEL

the anarchist.

You may have a good sense of humor, but that doesn't mean you put up with the things that go against your core values. Instead, you forge a path that will allow you to stand up for what you believe in.

Work it

You are powerful because you are:

- Fearless
- Secure in your values
- "Can do" attitude
- Hard-working
- Determined

Own it

Get inspired by these kindred brands:

Miley Cyrus - NYX Cosmetics

Bring it

Amplify your strengths:

- To ensure people don't see your wit as undirected, take time to come up with your core values and be sure to communicate them to your audience.

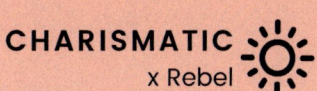

Your Brand Mix Mastery:

 CHARISMATIC x BFF

the congenial.

You see the value of coming together and encourage others to use their strengths in a way that benefits the greater good. You are often the first to volunteer for tough tasks, and you have every bit of confidence that a solution is possible if you work as a team.

Work it

You are powerful because you are:

- Peacemaker
- Recognize others' strengths
- Can-do attitude
- Present
- Positive

Own it

Get inspired by these kindred brands:

Fabletics - Drew Barrymore

Bring it

Amplify your strengths:

- People love you because you're one to talk everyone else up before yourself. Find and be vocal about that special something in everyone around you and you'll encourage others to do the same.

CHARISMATIC x BFF

Your Brand Mix Mastery:

☀ CHARISMATIC x 💎 GEM

the crystal.

You use positivity and a healthy dose of humor to fix tricky situations — and even to improve the ones that are already okay. Your optimistic nature reminds everyone to go easy on themselves.

Work it

You are powerful because you are:

- One to find a silver lining in every situation
- Lighthearted
- Playful
- Great problem-solving skills
- Tasteful

Own it

Get inspired by these kindred brands:

Ellen - Super Soul Sunday

Bring it

Amplify your strengths:

- As the old saying goes, "if you don't have something nice to say, don't say anything at all." You know you are most effective when you make people feel good, not bad.

Your Brand Mix Mastery:

the humorist

You are always ready with a joke and take every opportunity to make others laugh. You love using your creativity to put a smile on someone's face. When you're not actively lightening up a room, you're already coming up with ways you can in the future.

Work it

You are powerful because you are:

- Original
- Creative
- Observant
- Lively
- Ardent

Own it

Get inspired by these kindred brands:

Amy Poehler - Overheard LA

Bring it

Amplify your strengths:

- Don't waste time on those who don't appreciate or get your humor. Focus on your core audience in order to really hone your craft and build your tribe.

CHARISMATIC
x Original

Your Brand Mix Mastery:

☼ CHARISMATIC x ☼ CHARISMATIC

the comic.

Your brand is 100 percent Charismatic at heart. You're known for your good humor, which gets people through even the most harrowing situations. You're all about getting a laugh; no one is safe as a potential butt of a joke (including yourself).

Work it

You are powerful because you are:
- Funny
- Unique
- Confident
- Able to laugh at yourself
- Lighthearted

Own it

Get inspired by these kindred brands:

Betty White - *The Onion*

Bring it

Amplify your strengths:
- Go there, where others wouldn't dare. It keeps your material fresh and unexpected.

HOLLAH!
Bonus: Headshots 101
Find the tips at:
orangeandbergamot.com/bonus

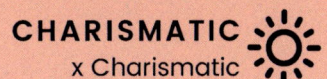

IRL INFLUENCE*HER*

Roxy Te

Founder, Society Social
Co-Host, HGTV's *Carolina Reno*
@societysocial

Photo credits: Elizabeth Shrier
& Lawrence Te

WHY WE THINK ROXY IS A PERFECT CHARISMATIC:
Roxy is a rockstar business owner and TV host with a knack for not taking it all too seriously. She not only infuses color and fun in her style and products, but her charm and humor come through in everything she does. (But don't take our word for it; you'll love her too!) shopsocietysocial.com

What makes you excited about your work?
Furniture and design if done thoughtfully and intentionally can add to the quality and value of home life. I truly love helping people create homes that they will be excited to share with their loved ones for years to come!

Can you share any struggles and how you've overcome them?
I find keeping up and trying to stay relevant amongst the growth of big retailers/e-tailers with deep pockets is always intimidating and daunting. To stay focused, inspired, and on track, I find being true to our brand and maximizing the strength of our furniture factories, makes the task more manageable, not to mention fun! Also, it doesn't hurt to have an amazing team!

Who is your muse?
My daughter! Watching her grow inspires me every day. With just her smile, she pushes me to be better in all aspects of my life. I want her to know she can do anything she puts her mind to and I want to be able to create a beautiful life for her in every sense of the word!

What's next for you?
After 7 years in business, honing our line and putting all our focus on building a retail recognizable brand, I'm excited to share that Society Social will be showing for the first time ever at the High Point Market trade show this October. We'll be showcasing 13 never-before-seen furniture designs along with our tried-and-true best sellers! Our team is so pumped to explore this part of the business and to round out our brand presence!

Words to live by:
My own made up mantra:

"Be grateful. Do good. Be kind. Skinny dip!"

...in other words, don't forget to have some fun along the way!

archetype speak.

Often you'll find in work and life, you're not speaking the same language as the other archetypes...either they tune out or misunderstand or it's just not getting through. Here's our guide to help translate how your fellow brand bosses *actually* communicate.

 Mavens...like to know what you're looking for so that they can provide you with something useful. Be prepared to ask questions related to their expertise. (And say thank you; maybe later express how you've used their advice...you'll make their day.)

 Brilliants...typically prefer not to use a lot of fluffy adjectives and feeling-words in communication. Cut to the chase. Well-organized lists and bullet points with supporting data is what they crave.

 Originals...want to feel as if they've had time to really brainstorm and explore all options before making a decision. Either provide them with options, or give them time (and a deadline) to come up with some their own.

 Idealists...are sensitive to negativity (how they would view straight talk). Start with the positives, and address areas of improvement as "opportunities for growth." Show your confidence in them.

 Gamechangers...are already three steps ahead in making their ideas reality before you even hear about it. Express your concerns but know that they've got to test it out for themselves first. They'll be full speed ahead so check in with them for progress updates.

 Explorers...are all about the journey and an abstract idea of the destination. Leave something to the imagination to keep them interested on the path you'd like them to follow.

> *HOLLAH!*
>
> **Bonus: Archetype Preach!**
> What do the other archetypes have to teach us? Get the tips:
> *orangeandbergamot.com/bonus*

 Powerhouses...like to make bold proclamations and be the top dog in most situations. If you can give them the space to do so in a few select areas, they'll feel, and perform at, their best.

 Bosses...enjoy feeling like they're accomplishing something, anything. They despise wasting time. Make sure they get to check off tasks (even small ones) towards a larger goal. And get your tasks done too; they'll respect you for it.

 Rebels...love to question everything. And be prepared that they won't accept your answer at face value. Better to present them with a painpoint and your thoughts, and let them come to the rescue with solutions of their own.

 BFFs...are very service-oriented. They like to know that you feel you can rely on them. But they value the same from you. So do what you say you'll do, keep them posted, be consistent and reliable.

 Gems...want to help. They need to feel useful and appreciated. Take time to tell them or show them how they've done so and thank them. Ask them how you can help too (but know they will decline...it's the gesture that counts for them).

 Charismatics...are the ultimate people-wooers. They live to win you over. They're not ones to dwell on negative situations, so if you're looking for someone to commiserate with you, you're looking in the wrong place. Crack a smile for them. Just be happy and you'll make them happy.

About the Authors

Kalika Yap

Kalika Yap is a serial (concurrent) entrepreneur whose businesses include an award-winning brand agency Citrus Studios, Luxe Link, the Waxing Co., the Tangerine Co. and Orange & Bergamot. Her companies have been featured in publications such as *Entrepreneur, Inc.., Wall Street Journal, LA Business Journal, The Huffington Post, The Today Show, CNN, MSNBC, Business Rockstars* and Microsoft's Entrepreneurship Week.

A native of Honolulu, Hawaii, Kalika started out working as a journalist for CNBC and Bloomberg after graduating from NYU, before making the move to the West Coast.

Kalika recently served as president of the Los Angeles chapter of the Entrepreneurs' Organization (EO), is a graduate of EO Entrepreneurial Masters Program (EMP) at MIT, and is the host of the podcast *Wonder*, ranked #7 for entrepreneurs by Inc.com. She has been honored by several organizations including the Asian Business Association, LA Business Journal, and the National Association of Women Business Owners (NAWBO).

Kalika spends her off time with her husband Rodney Yap and their two daughters Malia and Kailani enjoying life in their hometown of Pacific Palisades, California.

Erika Brechtel

Since 2002, Erika Brechtel has worked with clients around the world to create unique brand identities that empower female founders. Featured in *SELF* Magazine, *The Huffington Post, Refinery 29, Adore Home, The OC Register*, and on the cover of *OC Family Magazine*, Erika also contributes hosted content and interviews, leads workshops, and speaks at events.

Erika originally hails from the North Shore, Oahu, Hawaii, and received a magna cum laude degree at UCLA while playing on the first NCAA Division 1 women's soccer team there. Giving back has been a fundamental part of her life, volunteering for local and global organizations, most recently on the Board of Directors of the Junior League of Orange County, California (JLOCC).

Erika's greatest joy is being mom to her daughter Leighton, and living a grateful life together in Pacific Palisades, California.

I'm a *Boss*

I'm a *Maven*

In 2016, Kalika and Erika joined forces as Founder and Co-Founder of Orange & Bergamot, commited to providing 1 million female founders with the support and tools to succeed in business and create abundance for themselves, their families, their companies, their employees and customers.

Find out more: orangeandbergamot.com

> **You've always had the power, my dear.**
>
> *Glinda the Good Witch*

Made in the USA
Middletown, DE
05 September 2018